Jewish South Florida

Jewish South Florida

A History and Guide to Neighborhoods, Synagogues, and Eateries

Paul M. Kaplan

PELICAN PUBLISHING COMPANY
GRETNA 2017

The word "Pelican" and the depiction of a pelican are trademarks of Pelican Publishing Company, Inc., and are registered in the U.S. Patent and Trademark Office.

ISBN: 9781455622139
E-book ISBN: 9781455622146

Printed in the United States of America

Published by Pelican Publishing Company, Inc.
1000 Burmaster Street, Gretna, Louisiana 70053

To two special people:
Barney Pearson and Laura-Jeanne Monahos

Contents

	Preface	9
	Acknowledgments	13
Chapter One	History of Jews in South Florida	15
Chapter Two	Miami Beach	47
Chapter Three	Miami	109
Chapter Four	Broward County	145
Chapter Five	Palm Beach County	171
Chapter Six	Snapshot Profiles	199
Appendix	Suggested Videos	210
	Notes	211
	References	218
	Index	221

Preface

The story of Jews in South Florida is a fascinating one about which surprisingly little has been written. Though the area's history is short, it is rich in colorful characters, intriguing places, and unique architecture. The Jews of South Florida are a mosaic of different cultures. Many hail from Cuba and other Latin American countries. Others are retired Ashkenazi Jews, mainly from Northeastern states, who bring with them their culture, culinary preferences, arts, and religious practices. Historically, the area has been home to many survivors of the Holocaust. Still others are Sephardic with ancestral roots in Spain or Turkey. By the early 1960s, many Cuban Jews, both Ashkenazi and Sephardic, settled the area. Other Jews lived in rural Florida and served as farmers, distributers, or merchants. There are many stories to be told.

Think of this book as a compilation of the area's Jewish history, culture, and key people and places. It focuses on three counties: Miami-Dade, Broward, and Palm Beach. Read through the history of the region and learn about the Jewish role in its unlikely development in the late nineteenth century through the present day.

Once you read the history section, peruse the travel section. I recommend that you read the stories and interesting backgrounds of these places, particularly those you may not be familiar with. The write-ups incorporate not only secondary material but also quotes from archivists, curators, historians, synagogue administrators, shop and deli owners, and museum executives whom I interviewed in order to tease out a venue's often overlooked history, significance, and relevance to the public.

Readers sometimes ask why I chose to profile certain places over others. The book is not meant to be all-inclusive. Given this book's topic, I looked for venues related to Jewish culture. For synagogues, I focused only on historic ones. For museums and historic houses, I included those that were started by Jews and/or have at least some exhibits on Jewish topics. There is a separate section in each chapter called Other Significant Museums and Cultural Attractions; the historic houses, museums, and neighborhoods discussed in those sections do not have a direct Jewish connection but have nonetheless contributed greatly to the city's eminence. Often, their histories involve early settlers who interacted with the early Jewish pioneers. For eateries, I sought and sampled primarily Jewish-style cuisine. This includes New York style delis, Israeli and Middle Eastern food, Cuban cuisine, and contemporary food with a Jewish link.

I also searched for little-known places that offer rich experiences. For example, at the Jewish Sound Archives at Florida Atlantic University, you can listen to virtually forgotten, century-old music. Or you can watch the Klezmer Company Orchestra perform "re-imagined" century-old music usually with a new Latin American or Caribbean beat. There are largely Cuban or Turkish congregations. Their communal story of fleeing, settling, and thriving is key to the area's history. Still other places like the Miami Design Preservation League portray the area's architecture and preservation movements during the area's downturn. A Kabbalah Café in Broward County was also a unique find. It serves tea and holds events where philosophical and spiritual topics are brought to bear. Visiting the Holocaust Documentation and Education Center in Broward County is a poignant experience. These are just a few examples of what awaits you in this book.

There is also a practical element to the book. Entries in the travel section include logistical information. Because this frequently changes, check websites for the most current information. There are also Tips for the Traveler blocks that offer hands-on advice. Miami Beach is presented neighborhood by neighborhood, as the area is walkable within each distinct area. For Miami-Dade, Broward, and Palm Beach Counties, I do not call out different neighborhoods but rather the cities within a county, such as Fort Lauderdale, Hollywood, and West Palm Beach.

Part of reading a book like this is the visual experience. My hope is that through the book's contemporary and vintage photos, the area's history will come alive.

Behind the history and places are the lives of the residents. I profiled key individuals in the area's history, choosing them from different periods: nineteenth century, early twentieth century, 1970s, and contemporary. I also discuss a few famous non-residents with significant ties to the area.

In total, the book weaves together people, places, and stories to create a rich tapestry of the area's Jewish history and culture.

My advice is to read the entire book even if you are not going to all the sites listed. You'll be surprised by its history, people, and architecture and the little-known tales of many venues. Think of it as your guide to understanding and preserving the Jewish culture and history of South Florida.

Acknowledgments

I am grateful for the input and support from many who made this project possible.

Howard Brayer, a tour guide with the Jewish Museum of Florida and other institutions, was so generous with his time and insights. A huge thank you to Howard for all the walking tours and manuscript excerpt reviews. Even more, Howard gave me a framework for presenting Miami Beach's history. Howard is doing a stand-up job giving tours on a variety of topics to the public. Thanks also to both Aaron Davidson and Cindy Foster for their photography.

Many thanks to the Jewish Museum of Florida-FIU, including the executive director, Jo Ann Arnowitz, and Todd Bothel, the registrar and curator, for helping me acquire rights to photos. I also wish to thank Andy Gottliep of Temple Israel, Melody Torrens of Temple Beth David, Aaron Kula at Florida Atlantic University's Special Library Collection, and Shelly Isaacs at Café Cinematheque for their interviews. I was inspired by my interview with Rositta Kenigsberg, president of the Holocaust Documentation and Education Center, and was honored to meet with Rita Hofstradder, a longtime volunteer and executive committee member of the organization, and Stephanie Cohen, educational outreach coordinator. A special shout-out to Paul George, professor at Miami-Dade College, for his walking tour of downtown Miami.

I also salute individuals in New York City: Amy Stein-Milford and Hanna Griff of the Museum at Eldridge Street, Laurie Tobias Cohen and Lori Weissman at the Lower East Side Jewish Conservancy, and the Jewish Book Council for their partnership in promoting cultural history and experiences to the public.

A project as intensive as this is served by the support of family and friends. I am thankful to my parents, Jack and Eileen;

brother, Andrew Kaplan; uncle, Ted Katz; and cousins, Diane and Ed Ziegman and Robert and Jane Katz. May this book serve as an inspiration to my nephews, Kyle and Julian Rozanes, and their parents. I wish to also thank Barney Pearson for his close friendship and work on this book. My thanks to Laura-Jeanne Monahos for solid support and ideas. I also acknowledge the encouragement of other friends: Miguel Barrios, Jiyoung Cha, Paul Donnelly, Sharon Goldman, Olga Hopkins, Bonnie Kintzer, Jacob Koskimaki, Sumesh Madan, Ben Manalaysay, Angela Pruitt, Alfred Robert Hogan, Karen Seiger, and Felix Kaplan. I'm also thankful to the staff at Gotham Writing.

Finally, a shout-out to the team at Pelican Publishing: Kathleen Calhoun Nettleton, president and publisher; Nina Kooij, the talented editor in chief; Erin Classen, editor; Antoinette de Alteriis, promotion director; and Don Anderson, sales director.

Chapter One

History of Jews in South Florida

Jewish South Florida—one usually thinks of beaches, elderly Jews, and New York style delis. Yet a rich Jewish history and culture lies behind this surface.

In some ways, the story of Jews in South Florida is unique. The community of South Florida Jews is more recent, migratory, and Latino-influenced than that of other areas. Different ethnicities comprise the region's complex web of cultures. Some are part-time residents known as snowbirds. Many descend from post-Castro Cuba. Others hail from other Latin American countries including Colombia, Peru, Puerto Rico, and Argentina. The area is also one of the largest remaining residences of Holocaust survivors.

Today, the three counties of South Florida (Miami-Dade, Broward, and Palm Beach) comprise about 10 percent of the Jewish population in the United States (565,000), the third largest concentration after New York and Southern California. Of these, Miami-Dade has the fewest in number. Palm Beach has the highest percentage of Jews with 20 percent of households listed as Jewish. How did this trend start and develop?

Origins of Jews in South Florida

The ancestry of South Florida's earliest Jewish settlers can likely be traced to Spain. They practiced in secret in the midst of the Spanish Inquisition. During that time, non-Catholics were forced to convert or leave the country. It is theorized that a few sailed to the New World from Spain with Christopher Columbus in 1492. More followed in subsequent centuries. Spanish historian Salvador de Madariaga and other scholars surmise that Columbus may have been Jewish.[1]

The journey to Florida may have started as early as 1513 with Ponce de Leon's exploration of the area. Moreover, it is possible that the third Spanish governor of Florida may have been a Converso, or Jew who converted under Spanish rule.[2]

Though Conversos may have lived in the Spanish province of Florida from its discovery in 1513, none did so openly. Under Spanish rule, Jews were not permitted to settle in Florida.

Jews lived in Latin America during the 1600s and 1700s in varying periods of persecution and tolerance depending on who was in charge. After the Dutch and English conquered the Spanish in several cities, openly Jewish communities emerged. Examples were Curacao in 1634, Surinam in 1639, and Jamaica in 1655.[3]

The year 1763 marked a turning point. Spain lost Florida to the more religiously tolerant British. This transfer of power occurred with the Treaty of Paris, which ended the French and Indian War (1754-1763). This conflict was fought between the colonies of Britain and those of France along with Native American allies and was triggered by a dispute over the control for the strategically important Allegheny and Monongahela Rivers. At the war's conclusion, the British were given Florida while Louisiana was given to the Spanish. These changes brought feared restrictions. With their fate tenuous under the Spanish, many Jews decided to relocate to non-Spanish controlled areas.

Under this backdrop, three Sephardic Jews resettled from New Orleans to Pensacola in 1763. They likely wanted to flee Spanish rule and take advantage of the now more liberal laws of the British in Florida. They were Samuel Israel, Joseph de Palacios, and Alexander Salomon. There is speculation that Salomon was related to another Salomon who helped finance the American Revolution.[4]

Itinerant merchants, they purchased property and opened businesses there. Others joined, including Isaac Mendes of Jamaica, who moved to Pensacola in 1766; Samuel Judah, who moved to Pensacola in 1767; and Isaac Monsanto, who financed his voyage by selling his slaves. These merchants leveraged a vast network of trade customers, supplying wood and other natural resources to key port cities such as Charleston, South Carolina, and Savannah, Georgia.

Yet their tenure was brief. At the conclusion of the American Revolution in 1783, Florida reverted to Spanish control. Jews, in turn, fled for what is today Georgia, South Carolina, and a variety of northern states. These merchants' new homes were linked to key points along the predominant trade routes at the time. They moved based on commerce; still others were influenced by communal factors, as they preferred to live within established Jewish communities.

But this time, Spain did not expel the Jewish residents. Their needs had changed. Now they needed and even encouraged settlers in the fledgling territory. Thus, they tolerated a small Jewish population. In subsequent decades, Jews trickled into northern Florida.

Little is documented about Jewish life in Florida from the 1780s through the 1820s. There are virtually no records in Ladino, Yiddish, or Hebrew. Given their very small numbers, it is unlikely that any significant cultural or religious organizations were formed.

Nineteenth Century

The growth of the Jewish community in South Florida parallels the development of the state. During the nineteenth century, with the exception of the commercial port of Key West, settlements were established primarily in the northern and central regions. Early settlers avoided migrating farther south due to the humidity, swamps, mosquitos, and natives unhappy that their land was potentially being threatened. Moreover, there were few economic opportunities to lure settlers. Agriculture and trade were limited in the southern region due to the poor land conditions and lack of commerce.

In 1821, Florida again changed hands. Eying its strategic location, the American government bought Florida for $5 million. Though the Industrial Revolution was shaping much of the newly formed nation (infrastructure advances like the Erie Canal linked New York's Hudson River to the Great Lakes, for example), Florida seemed like another world. Its tough terrain and yellow fever epidemics kept tourists, residents, and businesses away. But some saw potential.

It was during this time that the most famous character from Jewish Florida's early days emerged. Moses Levy was born in Morocco in 1782. His ancestors were expelled from Spain at the close of the fifteenth century and found refuge in Morocco, where many Sephardic Jews (of Spanish descent) settled. In Morocco, the family name was changed to Levy. By the beginning of the nineteenth century, Moses had moved to St. Thomas in the Virgin Islands to enter the prosperous lumber business. His partnership with his cousin Philip Benjamin was successful, as the demand for lumber soared in the growing United States, in Europe, and in Cuba. As commerce expanded globally, the need for wood increased exponentially. The successful entrepreneur moved to Cuba in 1816 and expanded his trading and supplying of commodities. He accumulated a sizeable fortune. By 1819, he turned his interest to central Florida near modern-day Gainesville.

While his venture in the Virgin Islands was commercial, his aim in this remote part of Florida was visionary. He sought a refuge for persecuted Jews that would come to be named Pilgrimage Plantation. Perhaps drawing from his ancestors who had once been persecuted, Levy sought a communal, multi-family establishment free of any negative outside influences. It was to be a utopian settlement. He corresponded with New York City-based Shearith Israel, the oldest North American congregation, about his plans. He also conferred with Beth Elohim in Charleston, South Carolina, and congregants in Philadelphia. Further, he conducted a public relations campaign of sorts in the European press. A letter from Moses Levy at the time shows his persuasive tactics. "I call on you as a religious person . . . for in helping the fallen House of Israel, you are really truly assisting the human race at large."[5]

Along with his son and five German Jewish families, Levy lived on the plantation and built a plantation house, residences for the families, a blacksmith shop, stable, sugar mill, and corn house. By 1841, Levy had spent $18,000 to provide housing, food, clothing, and wages for participants.

But the dream was short-lived. Thirteen years later, the Seminoles destroyed the plantation during the bloody Second Seminole War. Amid political turmoil and challenging land conditions, the utopian ideal could not become a reality. Most settlers were from the city and knew little about rural living. Levy noted, "It is not easy to transform old clothes men [urban dwellers] into practical farmers."[6] Though Levy's vision was not realized, his ideas were remarkably progressive for their time. His projects and philosophies called for abolition of slavery, schools that were free and open, and a specifically Jewish school. He was a charter officer of the Florida Education Society.

By 1829, slavery was abolished in most northern states, including New York. But in southern states, it persisted. John Forester wrote in that year about Levy's prominence in the abolitionist movement: "Mr. Levy has by his conduct and discourses at meetings of Jews and Christians over his plan for the abolition of Negro slavery, made his name so well-known as to render further introduction of him to public notice unnecessary."[7]

Moses looked to his son, David, to carry on both his political and religious philosophies. He sent David to Norfolk, Virginia, in 1819 to receive a rigorous education. In the ensuing years, his son carried on this pioneering tradition. David Levy became highly active in politics and helped draft the new state's constitution. He represented the Territory of Florida in 1841 in Congress, where he argued for the merits of statehood. On March 3, 1845, his dream of Florida receiving statehood became a reality.

David Levy faced discrimination but was still elected to the US Senate when Florida became a state. His political philosophies— secession, states' rights, and slavery—aligned with those of white, Southern, agricultural interests.

Levy also helped build the first railroad across the state, a move that would forever change the formidable landscape. Named the Florida Railway, it connected the Atlantic Ocean to the Gulf of Mexico. The railway was championed by merchants and traders who wanted to expand their routes and speed up their time to market. It also provided a safer mode of transportation, less prone to theft. It drove down costs as the typically large shipping fees and taxes were diminished. For his accomplishments, a county and a town were named in David Levy's honor. Political success was shared in Levy's extended family as well; in 1852, his cousin Judah Benjamin was elected to the US Senate from the nearby state of Louisiana.

As the nineteenth century progressed, the United States was rapidly changing. Immigration surged. The Civil War deeply divided the nation, and transportation was made over by the Transcontinental Railroad. Though these changes swelled Jewish communities in southern cities like Atlanta and prosperous Charleston, the Jewish population in Florida remained small. By 1857, the eastern city of Jacksonville recorded the beginnings of a Jewish community, including the building of a cemetery. A few Jews also appeared in towns in northern and central Florida like Orlando and Pensacola. Most were peddlers with pushcarts of clothing, food, or other goods. Others who advanced economically had their own small retail stores.

Many early Jewish settlers in Florida were Sephardic. Like previous settlers, they usually resided in northern and central Florida. Some were descended from medieval Spain. For example, Alfred Wahnish's ancestors lived in Spain during the fifteenth century. After the Spanish Inquisition of 1492, his family migrated to England, likely through the Netherlands. It is speculated that they were Conversos, or New Christians—Jews who converted to Catholicism to avoid persecution yet still had to flee due to their ancestry. This family then took the anglicized name Wahnish, a somewhat common practice. Generations later, a descendant migrated to North Africa, where Alfred was born. He, in turn, immigrated to the United States via Boston. Years later, he moved to northern Florida and then, in 1890, farther south to the Tallahassee area, where he established a tobacco farm. The family's story exhibits typical migration patterns.

As the Civil War raged in the 1860s, many Jews in Florida sided with the South. They viewed slavery not as an ethical question but one of property rights. Jews from Pensacola, Ocala, and Jacksonville fought for the Confederacy. The exception was Key West, where Jews were more loyal to the Union.

Judah Benjamin became the treasurer and secretary of state of the Confederacy. In fact, in 1864, Benjamin was featured on the Confederate two dollar banknote. By May 1865 when the Confederates were all but defeated, Benjamin made a daring escape from the oncoming Union troops. He disguised himself as a farmer, hid, and eventually fled on horseback to Cuba en route to Europe. David Levy, however, had a different fate. The Union troops arrested and imprisoned him for more than a year at Fort Pulaski. He was later pardoned.

Florida's economy was devastated by the Civil War. In the ensuing years, trade recovered slowly. Religious and social organizations were introduced. In the 1890s, the Jewish population of Florida was about 2,500. In 1878, Beth El Congregation in Pensacola received a charter from the state as the first Jewish congregation and even had an organist. By the end of the century, there were five other congregations in Florida: Ahavath Chesad in Jacksonville in 1882; Rodeph Sholom in Key West in 1887; United Hebrews of Ocala in 1888; Schaarai Zedek of Tampa in 1894; and B'nai Israel, the second in Pensacola, in 1899. Many congregations adopted classical Reform rituals and customs that were more familiar to Protestant worship.

During this time, some European immigrants arrived in Florida. Many were from Husi, Romania. Some settled in Key West—by accident. Joseph Wolfson was aboard a ship that foundered off the coast of Key West in 1884. Fortuitously, he stumbled upon a small Jewish community. He made arrangements for the remainder of his family to join him in this new land. Others followed. Soon after, families from Eastern Europe and Russia settled in cities along Florida's coast.

Many were traditional peddlers. But a new industry that employed many Jews was emerging in Key West: the production of cigars. The industry magazine *Tobacco Leaf* published an article in 1885 called "Rush to Key West." Key West transformed the cigar industry by offering new popular products: "American" Cuban cigars. By 1888, Key West included some 129 cigar factories and had produced over 100 million cigars. Jews played a key role in this budding industry.

Some Jews were involved in smuggling prohibited items into the thriving island nation of Cuba. Through this illicit commerce, Jews and Cubans met. Many had similar political and business aims. Accordingly, some Jews were involved with the budding revolution in Cuba. Cuban revolutionaries who fled the island for Key West pleaded their case for freedom. Many in Key West, whose ancestors themselves had fled political oppression, were sympathetic. Each Sunday in Key West, the Jews "outfitted a donkey with basket panniers and led it through the streets where the donations to the Cuban causes were put in the baskets."[8] Jose Marti, a leader of the Cuban opposition movement, came to Key West to thank the Jewish community for its help.

Beyond fundraising, Jews in Key West played a key role in advocating for Cuba's independence during the Spanish-American War. Several lobbied for the cause where they could. Jews and Cubans both played a key role in this political advocacy as well as in the cigar industry. The two ethnic groups were united on this front.

Jews were involved in the building of Key West from its early days. In 1912, Jefferson B. Brown wrote in *Key West, the Old and the New*: "The Hebrews take much interest in the improvement and development of the town and are counted among the most progressive citizens."[9]

Though many had come from Yiddish-speaking families, they spoke a rudimentary Cuban-Spanish in addition to English. Many flourished, and anti-Semitism was not widespread. One theory to explain why is that Key Westers "were from the Bahamas and Cuba. They were adventurous and accepted people as they were, rather than on the basis of their origins and background."[10]

Yet the thriving, rural, and prospering Key West would transform when Henry Flagler pushed his railroad into Miami. The Key West landscape would be forever changed. No longer was Key West needed as a crucial port. Residents started leaving for other cities, like the burgeoning town of Miami. In ensuing decades, additional families departed Key West, a process accelerated by its economic decline.

Development of Miami

Largely uninhabited until the close of the nineteenth century due to its remote location from the more populated northern Florida, Miami sprang to life with the advent of the railroad. Along with other groups, Jews migrated to Miami. Jake Schneidman was the first known Jew to settle on the southeast Florida coast. He followed the railroad to West Palm Beach, where he opened his business. Sensing a larger opportunity in the new area of Miami, Schneidman moved there. In 1896, he opened the doors to his new shop, Biscayne Bay Dry Goods and Clothing Store.

On Schneidman's heels was Sam Singer, who set up two shacks near the railroad station as stores. Historical records show that his business was relatively prosperous, yet he remained in Miami for less than a year. His departure is a mystery. The next Jewish resident, Isidor Cohen, was the most famous of these three, arriving in 1896. Cohen was born in 1870. Following the recent pattern of Jewish immigration to northern states, he moved with his family to New York City at the age of thirteenth. His family was escaping the pogroms and violence that destroyed many towns. But Cohen was itching to leave the bustling metropolis for the South. So he dropped out of school and headed to Florida, where he opened a dry goods store in Fort Pierce. Soon after, he moved to Miami.

Cohen's journey was well documented in his *Historical Sketches and Sidelights of Miami, Florida*. He wrote in his diary in December

1896, "Miami looks like a real town. We have a City Hall, a jail, a volunteer fire department and water and light systems. Our merchants are doing a good business, derived chiefly from the building operations carried on by Henry Flagler and from railway employees."[11] Other Jews followed suit and moved to Miami to set up shops. Historians believe that Jews owned about 75 percent of the first sixteen retail stores.[12]

Advances in transportation would connect cities within Florida just as it had other parts of the nation. The railroad connected Jacksonville with more southern cities, ultimately reaching secluded Miami in 1896. Suddenly, the vast distance between cities was no longer an obstacle. The continued influx of immigrant Jews from Eastern Europe, which did not end until the Immigration Act of 1924, also increased settlers to Southern Florida by the early twentieth century. Moreover, the New York-based Hebrew Immigrant Aid Society directed some Jewish immigrants to Florida. Many of these settled in the state and soon after brought over their families from Eastern Europe and Russia.

With these infrastructure advancements, Isidor Cohen and Jacob Schneidman brought their merchant trade to modern-day West Palm Beach. Others settled in Miami, where there were

Joe's Luncheonette on Biscayne Boulevard, owned by Joe Perlman. Later, on Miami Beach, this became Joe's Broadway Deli. (From the collections of the Jewish Museum of Florida-FIU, originated by Marcia Jo Zerivitz, founding executive director.)

twelve Jewish merchants in 1896. Yet with the onslaught of yellow fever and a great fire in the same year, only two or three remained.

But its recovery was fast. By 1910, the general population of Miami had reached 5,500 and five Jewish families. Five years later, the number increased tenfold. In subsequent years, the Dixie Highway, which joined Miami with other cities, and a tourist boom and land speculation caused the general population to skyrocket. In 1925, 3,500 people of the city's total population of 130,000 were Jews. In the first decade of the twentieth century, some families moved directly from Russia and Eastern Europe to Miami.

The experience of Henry and Louis Seitlin showcased the increasing importance of Southern Florida to immigrants. The Hebrew Immigrant Aid Society sent Henry and Louis to a farm settlement in Homestead. The farm ultimately went out of business, so Henry sold shoes as a peddler. By 1912, he opened his own store, the hallmark of many immigrant peddlers' dreams. Achieving another common dream, he saved enough money to move his family with him. When Louis' wife died in 1912, there was no congregation cemetery in which to bury her. So her remains were taken to Jacksonville for a proper burial. This brought to light the urgent need for a congregation and local burial ground. That year, B'nai Zion was founded in Miami. After four years as a congregation, in 1916, a meeting was held at Sam Cohen's Lennox Hotel, where funds were pledged to purchase a lot. David Afremow contributed $5,000; he owned New York Bargain Store, one of the first department stores in Miami. The name of the congregation was changed from B'nai Zion to Beth David, under which it was incorporated in 1917.

World War I spurred economic activities in Miami and Key West. Many flying schools were established in Florida cities, including Miami. A large submarine and naval training station was located in Key West. Suddenly, Southern Florida began to receive national attention. Once the United States entered World War I in 1917, nearly two hundred Jewish Floridians served in the army and navy.

The New Frontier of Miami Beach

While Miami developed in the early twentieth century, the

unlikely development of Miami Beach started a little later. At the turn of the twentieth century, Miami Beach was described as a "wild strip of sand lined with dunes" and "forests of grapes and thickets of saw palmetto." Put another way, Miami Beach by 1913 was "little more than a reptile-infested, mangrove swamp, with palmetto scrub covering much of the narrow peninsula." The wild terrain was to be domesticated.[13]

Remarkably, only four decades prior, few knew of the island. In 1870, Henry Lum and his son Charles noticed a beach while sailing from Key West. They were intrigued. They decided to purchase the desolate island from the State of Florida in the deal of the century: $0.35 an acre. By the mid-1880s, the Lums thought about operating a coconut plant there. The natural habitat seemed like a suitable place. Soon after, Ezra Osborn and Elnathan Field of Middletown, New Jersey, purchased the land from the Lums for $0.75 per acre. The Lums walked away from the deal thinking they had profited handsomely on their investment. They had no idea what was to soon come to the island.

Osborn and Field set out to clear the land. Soon after, they ran out of cash. As a harkening to the frenzy of activity that would come, they sought investors. Osborn sold his share to an ambitious real estate developer, John Collins. Collins saw the agricultural potential in an island where a variety a tropical fruits could be harvested. While surveying, his sons saw great agricultural potential in this undeveloped land. They had no idea that the island would be a tourist paradise not long after.

But Collins' vision of transforming the island into a productive farm was soon changed by a midwestern developer named Carl Fisher. Fisher had amassed a fortune from other ventures. His goals for the island were less functional and more lofty. Rather than merely utilizing it for agriculture, he envisioned it as a tourist destination for the wealthy, trendy, and adventurous. He was impressed by the agreeable weather during the winter months and could foresee a demand from cold northerners looking for a more comfortable climate. Fisher knew how to "brand" the island— to showcase it as an exclusive destination with luxurious hotels, fashionable styles and picturesque beach scenes.

And so the grueling work of clearing the island began. Laborers hired from the Caribbean and elsewhere cleared mangrove swamps, dumped sand, and removed swarms of scrubs. Some of the most exhausting work was cutting, burning, and clearing the underbrush and dredging canals. Eventually, the work transitioned from removing what was there to developing the area's basic infrastructure. Workers built bridges, piers, and, eventually, houses. By early 1915, they had cut through a pathway, which would become Lincoln Road.

One of the earliest tourist attractions was a primitive two-story bathing pavilion on the ocean catering to Miami residents taking day excursions. Soon after, houses and casinos followed. Casinos were buildings for bathing and would often have restaurants and pools. They generally did not offer gambling, as the term may imply, but provided card games, swimming, and diving lessons.

In 1913, travel between Miami and Miami Beach would be forever changed with the construction of the Collins Bridge. It would become the longest wooden bridge in the United States. Political and business officials celebrated the opening of the bridge across the Biscayne Bay, allowing for easier transport.

Fisher utilized several marketing techniques to advertise the newly developed destination. These included publicity photographs, brochures, and postcards with enticing scenes. To heighten the drama of construction, Fisher also borrowed elephants from circus magnate P.T. Barnum and showed their use in the clearing of the land. He knew how to get the public's and the media's attention.

By the mid-twentieth century, despite the onset of the Great War (World War I), an optimism about this largely uninhabited land set in. One new resident wrote his relatives in Massachusetts, "Sell everything; come quickly to the land of milk and honey; you can walk down the streets and pick citrus."[14] Many responded to the call. They set out to take advantage of blooming job prospects. Opportunities for employment and entrepreneurship varied across industries from ranching, farming, and cigar making to the more traditional education, medicine, and law.

With World War I in the past, the roaring 1920s brought optimism, carefree spending, and lots of speculation. The nation was focused on style, building ever-taller buildings, and defying Prohibition (1919-1931). In 1920, women won the right to vote with the passage of the Nineteenth Amendment. America's population was swelling, and investors were looking for new opportunities beyond the over-speculated stock market. Indeed, the 1920s had such investing fervor that it was said shoe shine boys would give stock tips to their customers. F. Scott Fitzgerald's *The Great Gatsby* embodied these sentiments. Two industries blossomed: real estate and citrus farms. Previously vacant land was aggressively sold to land developers and tourists. Northerners flocked to the state to stake their claim. Irving Berlin's 1925 song "Florida by the Sea" for the Marx Brothers musical *The Cocoanuts* illustrated this movement. One verse includes the lines, "Buy a lot, any piece that we've got / Will increase ev'ry season," clearly referring to the promise that the value of land in Florida in the

Citrus label with "Florida" written in Yiddish, 1920. (From the collections of the Jewish Museum of Florida-FIU, originated by Marcia Jo Zerivitz, founding executive director.)

mid-1920s could only rise. (See chapter six to learn more about Irving Berlin and his ties to Florida).

The instant profits—at least on paper—attracted the interest of Jewish charitable organizations. The United Palestine Appeal (UPA), for example, raised significant funds, as did the American Joint Distribution Committee (JDC).

The boom reached its zenith in 1925. Crowds of garment manufactures, business people, doctors, lawyers, and retirees rushed to invest their hard-earned dollars in Miami and Miami Beach. (The years 2004-2007 would be eerily familiar, eight decades later.) This fervor gave rise to a new breed of investors called binder boys. Many were Jewish. Their proliferation and aggressive sales tactics fueled the housing boom, and may have contributed to anti-Semitism during this period. The booklet *Jewish Frontiersman* describes the phenomenon: "Dressed in the fashionable knickers of the day and in colors foreign to their northern life style, these men seemed to be released from their usual business cautions and inhibitions and eagerly placed binders on as many parcels of land as they could with the money available to them. These binders were deposits for which they received receipts and which spelled out the amount and sequence of the remainder of the purchase price."[15] But it was a scam of sorts. Had these binder boys been tasked to fulfill the contract terms, they could not have. All their money was invested in a series of binders, which were sold multiple times at a profit. It all seemed like a deal one could not pass up.

But then the music stopped. Several forces combined to undermine the vast expansion. A devastating hurricane in September 1926 dubbed the Great Miami Hurricane swept through the region, causing significant damage in South Florida. An account of the hurricane's aftermath describes its impact: "The next several days were punctuated by the wailing of ambulance sirens. Hospitals, badly damaged and often working by the light of lamps, attempted to treat the injured and dying. Those fortunate people who had candles used them for home lighting. Sterno was worth its weight in gold for cooking purposes. Most food was either spoiled or swept away. Everything was sodden and beginning to give off unpleasant odors, water for drinking or sanitation purposes was not available. Any vestige of hope for resuscitation of the boom were swept away by the hurricane."[16]

The hurricane was not the only problem. A fruit fly infestation ruined crops. The local economy was decimated. And by the end of the decade, the national economy collapsed with the stock market crash of 1929. Newspapers declared the area finished.

But the newspapers were wrong. By the mid-1930s, as the United States was slowly pulling itself from the grips of the Great Depression, Miami began its recovery. Tourists were lured by the weather, access to outdoor activities, and the region's newly proclaimed "Gateway to Latin America."

During this period, Jews faced significant discrimination, as did other ethnicities and races. Indianapolis-based developer Carl Fisher included clauses in land deeds prohibiting the sale of Miami Beach lots to Jews. Property deeds included covenants that barred both initial sales and subsequent sales to Jews. A letter from Fisher read, "No lot shall be sold, conveyed, leased to anyone not a member of the Caucasian race, nor to anyone having more than one quarter Hebrew or Syrian blood."[17] While this was more of an agreement of property owners and realtors than an actual law, and while some exceptions were made, its effects were widespread.

Prohibitions extended beyond land sales. Jews and other minority groups, such as African Americans, were not allowed to enter many of the area's key hotels. Numerous establishments hung Gentile Only signs at their entry. Some were coded with subtle phrases like Restricted Clientele. A survey revealed, "55% of hotels in Florida excluded Jewish patrons, whereas only 20% of hotels in Miami Beach did so."[18] Because of these restrictions, most Jews lived and conducted business below 5th Street in Miami Beach.

In a letter from the mayor of St. Louis, Victor Miller, to Fisher, Miller asked for "special permission for his Jewish friend to enjoy [Fisher's] golf course." The letter read, "One of the best friends I have on earth is staying at Miami Beach. He is the first person I ever played golf with. I realize that on account of his nationality there may be some objections but if you can possibly get him the courtesy of your golf club I shall be everlastingly grateful to you."[19] It is unclear what Fisher's response was.

Though there was significant discrimination against Jews, it was much less than in other areas of the United States. In many other states, a high percentage of resorts were completely closed off to Jews. For its time, Miami Beach was more liberal than many places.

Despite the general environment of intolerance, life south of 5th Street was bustling. Hotels catering to Jews in this neighborhood began to offer kosher food. In the late 1920s, Jewish activity pushed forward to Lincoln Road at 16th Street. Hotels thrived by catering to snowbirds and offering entertainment that competed with what clientele received in northern cities. Yiddish theater star Sophie Tucker and later comedian Jackie Gleason performed in night clubs and hotels. Miami Beach streets south of 5th Street were replete with kosher butchers, synagogues, and delis. Literary giant Isaac Bashevis Singer described his initial impressions: "Let me tell you, to me when I came here the first time, I had a feeling that I had come to Paradise! First of all the palm trees. Where would I ever see a palm tree in my life? Then, there was the fresh orange juice. That first sip was nothing less than ambrosia, especially after such a long journey." About the area below 5th Street, he remarked, "Here the sound of the Old World was alive as ever!" It was the "shetl by the sea."[20]

Some of the first Jewish services were held in 1925 in the David Court Apartments at 56 Washington Avenue (building no longer standing). Before that, Miami Beach Jews had to go to the city of Miami for organized services. By 1927, Congregation Beth Jacob, an orthodox synagogue, was formed and met in several buildings. In 1929, the congregation built 311 Washington Avenue, the first permanent synagogue in Miami Beach. In 1936, due to rapidly rising membership, the congregation built the building at 301 Washington Avenue and moved its main sanctuary there. The older building was used as a social hall.

Some may imagine this section like New York's Lower East Side. In fact, unlike New York's Lower East Side, the Jewish section in Miami Beach below 5th Street was not overrun with people. Industrialization and workers' rights struggles were far less an issue here than in northern cities. The economy in Southern Florida relied more on services, tourism, and agriculture than on manufacturing.

While the environment in South Florida was far different from that of the North, it benefitted from the gains in labor and healthcare made in northern states. Workers had more rights, patients had more access to healthcare and its improvement in treatments, and women had the right to vote. Reforms enacted by Jane Addams, Lillian Wald, Jacob Riis, Florence Kelley, and W.E.B. DuBois among many others paid dividends in this area. Their advances spilled over to South Florida.

The 1930s saw a shake-up in restrictions of Jewish purchasers of land. It was difficult to control after properties had a series of turnover owners. In addition, some sellers who wanted to unload their properties did not want to cut off portions of their market. Many owners were in great debt and urgently wanted to sell. During the downturn, Jews moved around the state to find business opportunities. By the early 1930s, Miami had overtaken Jacksonville as the city in Florida with the greatest number of Jews at five thousand.

Miami became more affordable and less aspirational during the Depression era. It was no longer the playground for the rich but became a destination for the middle class. During this period, Jews were elected to both citywide and statewide offices. Eleven served as mayors in cities such as West Palm Beach, Pensacola, and Tallahassee. David Levy Yulee, the first Jewish member of the US senate, had a descendant—Samuel Yulee Way—who served as mayor of Orlando for much of the 1930s. A lawyer from Daytona Beach, David Sholtz, was elected as Florida's twenty-sixth governor in the mid-1930s. Sholtz hid his Jewish identity to further his political career. He sang in an Episcopalian choir to deflect detractors. In 1934, Baron de Hirsch Meyer became the first Jewish city councilman.

By 1940, an estimated 20 percent of Miami Beach's population of 28,000 was Jewish. Most were concentrated below Lincoln Road.

With New Deal legislation, union workers received paid

Original Collins Fish Market owned by the Orlins. (From the collections of the Jewish Museum of Florida-FIU, originated by Marcia Jo Zerivitz, founding executive director.)

vacations for the first time. Many Jews from large northern cities, especially New York, were union members and thus could now afford a vacation in Florida.

Although some hotels and clubs were still restricting Jewish clientele, many did not. Quite a few hotels were built by Jewish developers, and Jews started to gain more influence in the city. In contrast to what had been there previously, new hotels were small, boutique-like, and fashionable. They were built largely on the roads closest to the ocean: Ocean Drive and Collins Avenue, the most sought-after locations. This gave rise to a "mini-boom" of building in what is now referred to as the Art Deco District. (See the architecture section of chapter two for more info.)

Besides hotel building, Jews were actively engaged in other industries. Many established banks, construction companies, and retail establishments. It was during this time that Sephardic businessmen and families settled in the area. They or their close ancestry often hailed from Greece, Turkey, North Africa, or Spain. Their first stop in the US was often New York City. It was here that many established commercial enterprises. Their ventures varied from the food business to agriculture to retail of women's clothing.

The Sephardic Jews tended to hold services apart from their Ashkenazi counterparts. Their rituals were different, as was their use of Ladino and their pronunciation of Hebrew. In Miami Beach, Sephardic worshippers changed locations until the congregation found a permanent one. By 1951, the Sephardic Jewish Center of Greater Miami opened. It served as a cultural center. There were often parties with belly dancers and Greek or Turkish music. It was said that everyone danced. Decades later, the population dwindled and the community center closed.

Miami Beach in World War II and After

World War II transformed the once-desolate Miami-Dade County. With the decision to station the Army Air Forces Technical Training Command in Miami Beach, armed services personnel from around the nation learned about South Florida. Department of Defense dollars also swelled coffers in Miami Beach. The army gradually "took over 85% of Miami Beach hotels with 25% of the Air Force officer candidates and 20% of enlisted

Wilfred "Wolfie" Cohen bought Al's Sandwich Shop at 23rd Street in Miami Beach during World War II, which became a popular spot. (From the collections of the Jewish Museum of Florida-FIU, originated by Marcia Jo Zerivitz, founding executive director.)

Soldiers in the Army and Army Air Forces marching on Lincoln Road in 1943. (From the collections of the Jewish Museum of Florida-FIU, originated by Marcia Jo Zerivitz, founding executive director.)

men training at Miami Beach."[21] Tourist destinations were converted to accommodate troops. The Miami Beach Municipal Golf Course, for instance, leased its land to the Army Air Corps for $1 per year. Restaurants were transformed into army mess halls. The "paradise for tourists" became a makeshift army base.

Jews in Florida were profoundly moved by the war. Many of their relatives had perished under the Nazis. Many watched along the coast of Miami Beach in 1939 as a boat with Jews fleeing Europe was denied entrance into the United States. One passenger, Herbert Karliner, later returned to the state, though his family had perished in the Holocaust.

As part of the war effort, many hotels with "restricted clientele" eased their policies and accepted Jews. African American recruits, however, were still largely separated. In 1949, a law was enacted that prohibited public signs that discriminated based on race and religion. But solid civil rights reforms were not enacted until 1964 under Pres. Lyndon B. Johnson.

After the war, many soldiers returned to the area, having taken a liking to its climate. Thanks to technological advancement in mosquito control and air conditioning, Miami's conditions proved hospitable. After the war, the opening of the airport and proliferation of cruise businesses enlivened tourism further.

It was during the 1950s, as the United States was growing exponentially with the baby boom, that Miami's population skyrocketed. In her book *To the Golden Cities*, Deborah Dash Moore notes the "three As" that drove post-World War II growth:

> *Army*—During World War II, Miami Beach became a large training facility for the Army Air Corps as no separate Air Force existed at the time. Many of the soldiers were Jewish, liked what they saw in Miami Beach, and returned after the war as vacationers, part-time residents (snowbirds), or residents including many retirees.
>
> *Airplanes*—Air travel greatly expanded after the war, and made Florida much more accessible.
>
> *Air-conditioning*—This technological advancement made the area much more livable year round. It also left behind those properties that were not air conditioned. Lower income residents were left in non-air conditioned homes.[22]

Miami's Jewish population grew along with it to about 70,000. Americans needed more space. Suburbs attracted growing families

Federation delegation to displaced persons in camp. From left to right: Rabbi Lehrman, Max Orovitz, and Fannie Selig, the first woman to visit displaced persons camps. (From the collections of the Jewish Museum of Florida-FIU, originated by Marcia Jo Zerivitz, founding executive director.)

disenchanted with traditional urban lifestyles. Builders were eager to meet this demand. It is estimated that in the early part of the 1950s, about 650 arrived to Miami each month. "A new house was built every seven minutes during this period, and many of the builders were Jewish."[23] Miami's first Jewish mayor was elected in 1952.

Two other groups of Jews came to South Florida during this time: survivors of the Holocaust in Europe and a portion of the estimated fifteen thousand Jews who fled Cuba.

The Jewish community became institutionalized during the post-World War II period, a change fueled by population growth and the need for new services. Newly formed social service agencies included the Jewish Federation, the Jewish Home for the Aged, the Sephardic Brotherhood of Greater Miami, a local YMCA, the Central Agency for Jewish Education, and many more.

Still, some lamented the lack of organization given the rapid growth and "permanent tourist" mentality. One observer noted at the time, "The community is still new, varied, and anxious to get ahead. It has no tradition of long standing so that the basic elements of ideological quarrels are missing or shelved in favor of a constructive job."[24] The sentiment was that "it appeared as though there was no unifying structure to hold the Miami Jewish community together."[25]

During this time, one character in Miami Beach was Meyer Lansky, who famously oversaw the mob's gambling operations in nearby Havana and Miami. Lesser known were his Zionist and literary interests. He wanted to move to Israel but was rejected by a wary Israeli government. Lansky was also a member of the Book of the Month Club and was said to have raised money for the new state of Israel from his casino operations. He recalled that he spoke to "some of the boys in Miami who were not known as generous when it came to making contributions. I told them this was the time to open their pockets, and open them wide. So you can understand why I am angry at the Israeli government."[26]

Many were drawn to the agreeable winter climate, lower cost of living, and easy-going lifestyle. A high concentration were elderly retirees who had worked in the garment industry and other light manufacturing. Now they wanted to enjoy their fixed-income pensions, many of which were earned through hard-fought labor reforms from decades prior.

To appeal to this demographic, marketers targeted Jewish

newspapers in the northeast. Miami Beach was called the "winter Catskill" or the "Borsht Belt of the South." These names referred to the popular resort community in upstate New York's Catskill Mountains. They were known for popular entertainment, food, and games. There was a thriving Yiddish culture in South Florida, including discussion groups and Yiddish theater. Famed writer Isaac Singer also retired to the area and contributed to its literary culture.

But after World War II, most of the housing and hotel development in Miami Beach was north of South Beach, in central and northern portions of the city. Newer hotels with entertainment, restaurants, pools, and air conditioning attracted postwar tourists looking for better amenities than were provided by the older hotels of South Beach. For example, the stylish Fontainebleau, built in the mid-1950s, cemented the image of Miami Beach as a place of style. Its founders—Ben Novack and his architect, Morris Lapidus—envisioned Miami Beach's reputation as the "winter playground for Jews in the United States." New apartments were also more appealing than the older housing stock of South Beach.

Despite these strides, discrimination persisted. Jewish physicians who were denied staff positions at area hospitals founded Mount Sinai Hospital.

While Jews were fighting for equal rights, the civil rights movement for African Americans began to accelerate in the late 1950s. The movement was sparked by the 1954 landmark case *Brown v. Board of Education* in Topeka, Kansas. African Americans began to attend previously segregated universities, but often with much harassment and threats.

Miami Beach played a role in the civil rights movement both for leaders and opponents. Alfred Stone hosted an African American Baptist convention at his Blackstone Hotel in Miami Beach in 1954. Sadly, this led to many death threats. Some rabbis throughout Florida, which was 30 percent African American by 1950, fought for civil rights. As a result, some congregations in Jacksonville and Miami were bombed. In fact, today Miami-based Temple Israel houses a cross burned by the Ku Klux Klan at this time.

Miami and Miami Beach in the 1960s to 1980s

Another major demographic shift occurred in the 1960s with

the arrival of Cuban Jews fleeing the the Communist takeover in 1959. About 3,500 Jews were exiled to the United States after Fidel Castro took over the island. By 1961, a total of about two-thirds of Jews in Cuba left due to disharmony with the revolution's ideology as well as from fears of discrimination or persecution. Many immigrated to Miami and the surrounding area. About 20 percent were Sephardic. Some remarked on the irony: "Look at how things turn out. We came to Cuba because it was the country closest to the United States. We came to the United States because it was the country closest to Cuba," remarked one exile to a *Miami Herald* reporter.[27] Most exiles preferred Miami due to its similar climate to their former country.

The new Jewish-Cuban immigrants faced challenges known well by other immigrant groups. They had to rebuild themselves economically, which in many cases meant doing work that was different from what they were trained in. In addition, they had to assimilate culturally to a community that was less than warm to their arrival. New arrivals felt shrugged off by the larger Jewish community. Many reported being "ignored" and "treated with indifference." Ironically, many of the "Jewbans" (Cuban Jews) were treated with the same disregard that the Jews already in the area had experienced a generation prior.

Their history was different from that of other Jews in South Florida. The Cuban-Jewish community had formed in the early twentieth century after the Spanish-American War. They varied from Sephardic Jews from Spain, parts of the Balkans, or Turkey to Ashkenazi Jews from Eastern Europe. Beside Spanish, other languages spoken ranged from English to Ladino to Yiddish. As was the case elsewhere, destitute Jews arriving in Cuba started often as street peddlers hoping to open their own stores. The environment was generally tolerant.

Though the larger Jewish community seemed inhospitable to their arrival, one exception was Rabbi Mayer Abramowitz of Temple Menorah. He offered free synagogue membership to the Cuban refugees. He provided an analysis of the situation to the *Jerusalem Post Magazine:* "The Jewish community did very little to absorb the fleeing Jews of Cuba. We thought they were wealthy and could manage. Second, the US government had a program to absorb all Cuban refugees so the Federation of Greater Miami

Welcome station established by the Cuban-Hebrew Congregation of Miami to welcome immigrants coming to Miami on Freedom Flights in 1965. (From the collections of the Jewish Museum of Florida-FIU, originated by Marcia Jo Zerivitz, founding executive director.)

did not get involved."[28] (See Temple Menorah in the following chapter.)

In response, many Cuban Jews split with existing Jewish congregations and established their own. The Cuban-Hebrew Social Circle was born. Its traditions mirrored those from the institution's earlier days in Cuba. As the population of Cuban-Jews increased, so did their standing. They could now worship and socialize with their shared culture rather than having to assimilate to the broader South Florida one. This movement yielded the Cuban Hebrew Congregation for Ashkenazi Cubans and Temple Moses for the Sephardic Hebrew congregation. Temple Moses also has congregants whose ancestry goes back to Turkey. (See the following chapter for more information on both synagogues.) Here, Sephardic Jews from Cuba reestablished their community in the region as well. Spanish and Ladino were spoken at religious services and at other functions. In ensuing decades, Sephardic Jews from other countries joined this community.

The 1970s and 1980s brought significant changes. Jews during this era emigrated from other Latin American countries, including Nicaragua, Argentina, Columbia, Brazil, and Venezuela. Their moves were motivated by their country's failing economic and political systems. Many chose to settle in Miami and the surrounding area due to its large Latino population and by-then vibrant Jewish community.

During this period, Miami and Miami Beach declined for a variety of reasons. The services-driven economy was sluggish. Drugs became a huge problem. Crime soared. Below 5th Street, the neighborhood was particularly bad. Many who could afford to move north did so. This was the era depicted in the hit TV show *Miami Vice*. Many Miami residents moved to northern counties like Broward and Palm Beach.

Miami Beach physically deteriorated. Some neighborhoods had boarded-up buildings, limited services, and few eateries. Many buildings became rooming houses for indigent residents. Much of the Jewish population was elderly and poor. Such South Beach neighborhoods were called "God's waiting room." It was hardly the area the original developers had imagined in 1915. It was supposed to be a tourist destination for the affluent.

But some real estate developers saw potential. Like Carl Fisher decades prior, they envisioned an aesthetic neighborhood with canals and shiny new condos. To accommodate this, most buildings below 5th Street were to be torn down to "beautify the area."

Like in other major metro areas, when the historic buildings were threatened, preservationists stepped in. Some were inspired by those who saved landmark buildings in New York City after the disastrous teardown of the once-monumental Pennsylvania Station. Barbara Capitman stepped into the preservation scene at this time. A Jewish designer from New York, she moved to Miami in 1973. Recognizing the unique architecture of the art deco, Mediterranean, and Miami modernist styles, she fought to save buildings.

Her efforts were institutionalized within a few years with the inception of the Miami Design Preservation League in 1976. The new organization founded the Art Deco Historic District and had several buildings preserved in the National Register of

Historic Places. This district encompasses most of South Beach, from 6th Street to 23rd Street and from the beach to just two blocks east of Biscayne Bay, a total of about ten blocks east to west. Importantly, placement on the Register did not protect old buildings. During the 1980s and 1990s, laws were gradually strengthened to make it harder to demolish or alter buildings in the district. There are 1,200 structures in the historic district, of which 1,000 are protected under current laws. Although buildings cannot be destroyed, the interiors may be altered.

But the area south of 5th Street was excluded from these preservation efforts. Developers were a powerful group. Though preservation efforts did not thwart their efforts, the economic downturn did. The early 1980s brought a severe recession, and building plans were postponed.

In the 1980s, Capitman's revitalization efforts were joined by Leonard Horowitz, a Jewish thirtysomething eager to help the cause. His approach was changing the visual color pattern of buildings. He developed a palette of colors to be used on art deco buildings to accentuate architectural details. The buildings were drab. Horowitz's efforts brought them to life. He borrowed colors from nature—the sky and sea. TV producers took notice. The hit TV show *Miami Vice* used many buildings as a setting for the show.

It was during the period of the 1950s to the 1980s that Miami Beach was its most "Jewish." To put this into numbers, by 1950, about half the Miami Beach population of 46,000 was Jewish. By 1960, approximately 60 percent of Miami Beach was Jewish, including approximately 80 percent of South Beach. This stands in marked contrast to the percentage of Jews in the national population during these periods. Following World War II, Jews were about 3 percent of the total US population. Currently, Jews are under 2 percent of the total US population. Exact percentages vary depending on definitions.

But after the 1980s, the Jewish population in Miami Beach declined markedly. In the mid-1990s, as the overall United States economy soared, South Beach gentrified. It became fashionable once again. Film stars, models, and fashion designers made the area trendy. The once shabby hotels were now colorful thanks to preservation efforts.

This revitalization brought a steep increase in prices. Many could not afford to live in the neighborhood any longer. Once inhabited by many lower income elderly Jewish from northern states, the neighborhood became only for the affluent. Efforts for low-cost housing were limited. Former residents moved in with their adult children or to cheaper areas. Others preferred a suburban environment in northern counties. Many passed away over time.

From April to October of 1980, the Mariel boat lifts brought a large influx of poor Cuban residents. It was spurred by a sagging Cuban economy and the surprising announcement from Fidel Castro that anyone who wanted to leave Cuba could do so. Organized by Cuban Americans excited to reunite with their relatives and friends, private boat companies and even individuals with makeshift boats began to bring Cubans across the waters to Miami.

Many on the boat lifts were upstanding individuals who have contributed to the US greatly. However, it was discovered that a number of refugees were former prisoners and residents of mental health facilities. This backfired on then-president Jimmy Carter. Unfortunately, the percentage of refugees who were criminals and drug traders soured the public taste for accepting and integrating Cuban refugees. This is portrayed in the 1983 hit film *Scarface*, a remake of a 1932 classic. With many criminals choosing to stay in Miami or Miami Beach, crime rose dramatically. The spikes in violent crime and drug use made the once comfortable area south of 5th Street more undesirable. This hastened the moving of many Jewish seniors who felt that their area was no longer safe.

Over six months, about 125,000 Cubans had sailed to the Sunshine State. Due to the "Open Arms Policy" of the Carter administration, Cuban refugees were granted citizenship and rights. It should be noted that later studies found that fewer than 5 percent were deemed criminals under US law and denied citizenship. It is theorized that Castro included undesirables in the refugees to hinder the image of Cuban exiles and to save money on jails and mental health facilities by pushing those residents to the United States. Still, the negative image created a public relations headache for the Carter administration.

1990s and 2000s

In the 1970s to 2000s, many Jews moved to Broward and Palm Beach. The median age of South Beach dropped dramatically to thirty-nine in 2010. Cubans and Latinos from other parts of Latin America comprised the majority of the population. Over time, more residents were foreign born and part-time. South Beach also became a prime area for gays and lesbians because of its plethora of bars, clubs, and community organizations. Many consider the mid-1990s through the mid-2000s to have been the prime years of gay life in South Beach. After that, many gay people moved north to cities like Fort Lauderdale. Some were likely priced out of the expensive market. Changing demographics and generational attitudinal shifts likely caused these changes. As a result, many South Beach bars closed.

In 2009 and 2010, the region was greatly impacted by the financial downturn. Particularly in Miami, the real estate market was greatly over-speculated from a buying fever. It was said that it looked as though "the [building] crane [was] once again the state bird in Florida."[29] Harkening back to the land speculation and grab of the 1920s, history repeated itself. Easy access to capital regardless of credit accelerated the buying frenzy. Then, in late 2008, the market crashed. Foreclosures and half-empty condos littered much of South Florida.

Yet, like decades prior, South Florida continues to recover from its downfalls. Today, it is a key destination for international visitors. The Jewish population in downtown Miami, Broward County, and Palm Beach County is on the upswing. In Miami Beach, it is largely concentrated around 41st Street with a bustling life of synagogues, yeshivas, kosher supermarkets, delis, and community centers. Miami Beach's Jewish population is about 15 percent of the total, or about 13,000 residents.

Recent years have also brought about demographic shifts. A 2014 Greater Miami Jewish Community study shows that the last decade has reversed the decline of greater Miami's Jewish population. Observers were surprised to see a 9 percent growth. Driving this increase is the 17 percent growth in residents under the age of thirty-five since 2004. More are moving downtown. Miami Beach, once the home of many older Jewish residents, now has a preponderance of children and young adults. But not all residents are thriving; the survey notes that 29 percent are "just managing" or "can't make ends meet." Miami-Dade also has one of the largest percentages of foreign-born Jews of any US community. Many hail from Cuba and other Latin American countries.

Counties north of Miami-Dade have other distinctions. Palm Beach County has the oldest median Jewish age in the US. The southern part of the county, which includes Boca Raton, has the highest percentage of Jews in the entire US population. In Broward County, mortality rates have decreased the Jewish population. Fewer retirees are moving to the area. Yet retirees are still choosing Palm Beach County to live during their golden years. The Orthodox community has grown most markedly in Miami Beach, Aventura, Boca Raton, and Hollywood.

Institutions are responding. To accommodate the population increases, new Jewish day schools, community centers, and synagogues have opened or expanded. Many are focusing on the needs of young families.

Development of Palm Beach and Broward Counties

Palm Beach and Broward Counties followed a similar trajectory to that of Miami. Land boomed, though on a smaller scale, in the mid-1920s only to be interrupted by the Great Miami Hurricane in 1926. The area fell into a deep economic slump several years before the Great Depression. These counties did not have the growth factors that Miami did, such as the World War II military stations and the large influx of Cuban and other Latin American immigrants. Therefore, Broward and Palm Beach Counties' growth was largely in the 1970s and later.

Growth in Palm Beach County was slow during its early years. Its population boom has mostly been in the latter half of the twentieth century. Harry and Florence Brown from Saint Louis were among the first Jews to reside in Boca Raton. It is said that this was a time when "it was still possible to sit in the middle of Old Dixie Highway and play cards."[30] The extended family opened Hutkin's Food Market, and Max was one of the founders of Temple Beth El, the first Jewish congregation in Boca Raton. (See chapter three for more on Temple Beth El of Boca Raton). Despite its humble origins, it is today one of the largest congregations in the area. The first Jews in West Palm Beach followed a similar pattern of opening a retail store and starting a congregation. Also, with a nod to the area's agriculture, one of the founders was a produce farmer, while another served as mayor of the developing town in 1923-24.

Much of the early businesses were on Clematis Street. On this street, early Jewish settlers started retail stores. These included "Joseph Schulpler's hat store, Cy Argintar's men's Shop and Toby and Selma Myers' luggage business."[31]

Broward County's history is best represented by the Stranahan House in Fort Lauderdale. Built at the turn of the twentieth century as a trading post, it is the oldest surviving structure in the county. At this time, the Seminole Indians camped at the post for several days. Several years later, Frank Stranahan and his wife, Ivy, built a residence on this site. Ivy was highly active in the Seminole Indian community. As a teacher, she informally taught the Seminole children and advised the tribe on key decisions about land use. Ivy would become one of the most influential women in Fort Lauderdale's early history.

By 1920, another house, which still stands today, was constructed: the Bonnet House. It is speculated the early Spanish settlers had contact with these grounds. The house itself dates to 1920, when the land was mostly wilderness. (See chapter four for more information on both houses.)

The oldest synagogue in Broward County is Temple Emanau-El. Its founding was auspicious; it started in a rented room above a restaurant on Andrews Avenue. The Hurricane of 1926 that ravished the area blew off the roof. In one day, it was gone.

Temple Emanau-El was founded by Moe Katz, a real estate salesman, who moved to the area in 1923 with his brother, Mack. The two brothers had helped organize the congregation.

Just as the area recovered from the hurricane's devastating wake, so did the new congregation. Services were moved to a new building on South Andrews Street. By 1937, it offered high holidays. By the late 1960s, the congregation Emanu-El of Fort Lauderdale moved to a new location.

That building, at South Andrews Avenue and 18th Street, celebrated its initial prayer services for the High Holy Days in 1937. It was the location for Emanu-El until 1968, when the members moved to the more central Lauderdale Lakes location. In 2004, it merged with nearby Kol Ami.

With the expansion of Fort Lauderdale and the surrounding

area, the temple spawned other area synagogues, including Beth El in nearby Hollywood and Bat Yam in eastern Fort Lauderdale. In the 1980s to 2000s, the Jewish population significantly increased. It is estimated that there were about one hundred synagogues built between Broward and Palm Beach Counties. Some are more vibrant than others.

Conclusion

Today, South Florida is a thriving area. In some ways, the area harkens back to the vision of Carl Fisher. It has become a tourist mecca. Miami Beach's demographics continue to change. More residents are from Cuba and other Latin American countries. Though there are fewer elderly Jews in Miami Beach, some of the culture remains. Miami is thriving with its gentrified downtown. Once withering Jewish congregations in downtown Miami have rebounded. In Broward and Palm Beach counties, some of the oldest congregations and historic houses remain. Though these counties have less early twentieth-century history than Miami and Miami Beach, they have notable museums, synagogues, and cultural centers from more recent decades. Other Jews have moved to other parts of the state, including Tampa, Sarasota, and Naples.

Now, we turn to the specific places of Jewish interest in these areas. We will look at the stories behind these places and many of the key people in the area's development. We will also explore their architecture, food, museums, synagogues, and memorials.

Chapter Two
Miami Beach

Early Jewish life in Miami Beach centered below 5th Street; generally, Jews were not allowed to purchase properties north of this area. With no synagogue, early settlers worshipped in Miami. The Jewish population of the newly developed island increased in the 1920s. Slick advertising and abundant lands invited many to move or visit the island. In 1927, Beth Jacob, the first congregation on Miami Beach, was formed. (It would last until 2005 when it sold its property to the Jewish Museum of Florida.) Yet the Great Hurricane later that decade curtailed this rapid growth. By the 1930s, the region was recovering and discrimination was abating, leading more Jews to move into Miami Beach. Large numbers of Jews bought land from debt-strapped owners hoping to unload it. Jews also played a key role in the art deco movement of the 1930s and '40s.

Many Jewish soldiers discovered Miami Beach during World War II, as it was a key military training center. After the war, many decided to stay. Jewish doctors, unable to find work at hospitals in the area, formed Mount Sinai in Miami Beach. By the 1950s and 1960s, air conditioning, mosquito control, and the automobile brought droves of tourists and new Jewish residents. About 650 Jews arrived in the area monthly. Snowbirds from northeastern states often lived in Miami Beach during the winter months. Synagogues and restaurants catered to this surge, and the area became a mecca for Jewish middle-class retirees. It also became the home of many Holocaust survivors. Many Cuban Jews, known as "Jewbans," fleeing Fidel Castro's Cuba lived in Miami Beach. Their reception by other Jews, though, was mixed. Later, Jews from other Latin American countries moved to Miami Beach. During this period, Jews increasingly moved to North Miami and North Miami Beach.

However, during the 1970s and 1980s, the area began to fall

into disrepair. Many Jewish retirees chose Broward County and, in subsequent decades, Palm Beach County. Crime soared. Jewish preservationists like Barbara Capitman fought to keep art deco buildings intact. Many elderly Jews died while others moved away. Yet Miami Beach's Jewish community thrived with the arrival of Jews from Israel, Russia, and Latin America.

Recent decades have seen a rejuvenation of the once idyllic island. Jewish life flourishes in many neighborhoods in Miami Beach. Its history is captured in historical eateries like Joe's Stone Crab and in relatively new museums like the Jewish Museum of Florida, the largest of its kind in the state. Other remnants of the past are no longer: famous delis like Rascal's and Wolfie's have closed. Still, new delis have since popped up. There has been a resurgence of Orthodox and Chabad Jews, particularly in the northern parts.

Today, there is a wealth of sites to visit. Though known for its lush beaches, ornate hotels, and parties, Miami Beach also has a history and culture waiting to be explored. Walk in the old Jewish neighborhood below 5th Street. Visit the four museums. Take an architecture tour and learn about the enduring work of preservationists. A visit to the Holocaust memorial is a must. Read about the old, famous delis and dine at some contemporary ones. Explore art and cultural museums like the Wolfsonian and the risqué World Erotic Art Museum. And maybe catch some sunshine and ocean waves along the way.

Miami Beach Architecture

Architectural history is intertwined with the development and preservation of Miami Beach. The area is known for three basic architectural styles: art deco, Mediterranean revival, and Miami modernist. Read their defining characteristics below. If you would like more details and examples, I recommend the exhibits and tours of the Miami Design Preservation League.

Art Deco

It's a term that seems interchangeable with Miami Beach. It's hard to read about the city's history or architecture and not see it come up repeatedly. But what exactly is art deco architecture?

It's probably more of an aesthetic movement than a tightly defined architectural style. Popularized in Paris during the roaring mid-1920s, it gained steam during its exhibit at the International Exposition of Modern Industrial and Decorative Arts in France. Other countries took up the form from the late 1920s until World War II. Therefore, art deco is not limited to Miami Beach. It was a global movement. A noted example in New York City is the Chrysler Building, which was built during this time.

In Miami Beach, many buildings erected during the 1930s and 1940s were part of the worldwide "second wave" of art deco known as streamline moderne. Less decorative and more modest, the movement reflected the Great Depression, during which many of its buildings were constructed. It's playful yet grounded in symmetry. Some of its decorative elements are whimsical flora, fauna, and ocean-liner motifs. Motion and speed are evoked. Building exteriors contain stepped rooflines, a defined symmetry, and "eyebrow window overhangs," or sunshades over windows designed to reduce angles of the hot Florida sun. Also designed to shield residents from nature are the characteristic porthole windows, reminiscent of 1930s ocean liners, and relief facades. Some art deco buildings also have neon lighting, and often their edges and corners are curved rather than linear.

Art deco boutique hotels punctuate Ocean Drive. An example is the Breakwater Hotel on Ocean Drive and 9th Street. It has a defined symmetrical design yet is streamlined. It's colorful, and its façade features the stepped, ziggurat pattern characteristic of the art deco movement. Another example is the Carlyle on Ocean Drive, in business since 1941. Art deco is showcased through the rule of thirds, whereby the vertical section is divided in thirds. Film buffs may recognize this building from *Scarface* (1983) with Al Pacino—a remake of a 1932 classic—and *The Birdcage* with Robin Williams (1996).

Built in 1935 for Paramount, the Colony Theatre exhibits noteworthy art deco elements like its marquee, façade from the restored ticket box, and the geometric patterns in the terrazzo flooring.

Mediterranean Revival

Think of it as a trip back in time to Greece or Spain during the

The Breakwater Hotel on Ocean Drive, showcasing art deco architecture. (Photo by Aaron Davidson.)

The Congress Hotel in quintessential art deco style on Ocean Drive. (Photo by Aaron Davidson.)

Renaissance period. Probably the best-known characteristic is the red tiled roofs. Structures usually have a rectangular floor plan and large, symmetrical exteriors. Multiple hip roofs are on multiple levels to create visual appeal. Arches are utilized to emphasize entryways, courtyards, and windows. The style evokes an Old World image. Some also have loggia, archways that create a corridor between the building and open courtyard. Other notable features are "decorative columns, arched windows, clay barrel roofs, rough stucco walls and spindle gates guarding picturesque courtyards."[1] Some have curved archways. The stucco is often textured with a mix of cement, water, and lime or a similar material. This makes the surfaces appear more "Old World."

This look was popular in the 1920s and 1930s. Espanola Way in South Beach showcases quintessential Mediterranean revival structure. Famous examples in the area include the Villa Vizcaya in Miami and the Boca Raton Resort and Club in Boca Raton.

Miami Modernist (MiMo)

Two decades after the zenith of the art deco and Mediterranean revival movements, Miami Beach was a different place. World War II ended. Miami Beach was put on the map. Residents were moving to the suburbs. With the proliferation of modern art, artistic movements were likewise changing. A new optimism and hope for the future set in. This was reflected in the Miami modernist movement.

Some compare this style to the grace of the automobile: "Automobiles with soaring fins tacitly sliced through the air with graceful ease; sparkling new appliances promising to alleviate housework appeared in every kitchen."[2] Design elements like "eyebrows" were replaced by sun shades, tiled mosaic walls, and metal louvers. Open balconies and catwalks became prominent features. The style has a futuristic sensibility in space-age forms as well as a glamourous vibe suggestive of material excess.

Two classic examples in Miami Beach are the famed Fontainebleau Hotel and Eden Roc, both built by Morris Lapidus. Part of the area near Biscayne Boulevard is called the MiMo Biscayne Boulevard Historic District, or the "MiMo on BiBo."

Miami Beach—Below 12th Street

Museums

Jewish Museum of Florida-FIU
301 Washington Avenue
Phone: (305) 672-5044
Website: https://jmof.fiu.edu
Hours: Tues.-Sun., 10 a.m.-5 p.m.
Admission: $6 adults

The Jewish Museum of Florida has an interesting history. Founded in 1927, it began as a thriving synagogue for Congregation Beth Jacob. This neighborhood below 5th Street was a small "Jewish ghetto" of sorts. Most Jews could not live or stay in hotels north of 5th Street at the time. By 1929, the growing congregation had built the structure at 311 Washington Avenue. The timing was inopportune—it was during the heart of the Great Depression.

The synagogue's significance cannot be overstated. Prior to the mid-1920s, Jews were not permitted to build synagogues. They had to travel across the Biscayne Bay to worship. During the recovery of the 1930s, the congregation continued to grow. Art deco architecture was the rage. The congregation built a larger building next door at 301 Washington that was designed by the famed architect Henry Hohauser, the "father of art deco." This was an early work in what would become a prolific career. (See page 62 for a partial list of his projects.)

The original building became the social hall, while the new one housed the sanctuary. The new building contained many colorful stained-glass windows, art deco chandeliers, and, in Miami style, a marble bimah and a copper Moorish dome. An orthodox synagogue, it had a women's balcony.

Builders of the synagogue employed a little-used architectural trick: to allow all worshippers to see without other congregants blocking their view, the seating was sloped.

The museum's literature describes the cost, construction, and significance of the new synagogue. "The central double door of 301 Washington Avenue has inset panels, highlighting the Star of David. The main entrance is elevated by ten steps surfaced in tile and is approached from three sides. Above the door is a large arched stained glass window that represents the giving of the Ten Commandments to the Jews on Mount Sinai with the rays of the Divine presence streaming down from the clouds. The entrance is flanked by coupled fluted pilasters of cast stone, topped by composite capitals with the fluting continuing in the arch."[3]

These were the days before air conditioning. A battle of sorts was fought between opening the window and hearing street noises versus stuffiness and humidity inside the building. To compete with the street noise, it is said that the rabbi had to speak "so loudly that he could be heard a block away. The sun shone so brightly that it was impossible for the worshippers to read their prayer books."[4]

For decades, the congregation and the two-building synagogue thrived—until they didn't. By the 1970s and 1980s, the neighborhood was deteriorating. Crime soared. Elderly Jews were moving away. This change devastated the congregation. Ultimately, the building was abandoned and became dilapidated.

Mother Nature did not help. The powerful Hurricane Andrew in 1992 destroyed the roof, allowing water to ruin the once-beloved interior. The building was further harmed by vandalism. Its future was in grave doubt.

Yet another force was in play that would change the future of the once thriving building. MOSAIC was an organization looking to collect and disseminate Florida's Jewish history. It was like a mosaic tile in a larger mosaic picture. At first, it was to be a traveling exhibit throughout the state and other US cities.

But then organizers decided to make it permanent. It needed a new home. By 1993, it was eyeing the buildings. The organization decided to house a new museum of Florida Jewish history in the now-dilapidated structure. The process was brutal and laborious; preserving the integrity of the original architecture made it particularly difficult.

By 1995, the restoration was completed and the museum opened in the 1936 building. Though the neighborhood had begun to gentrify, the congregation continued its precipitous decline. By 2005, there were scarcely any members. The congregation—which was the first in the neighborhood—disbanded.

Once Congregation Beth Jacob, founded in 1927, this building is now home to the Jewish Museum of Florida-FIU, one of the key museums in the area. (Photo by Aaron Davidson.)

By 2005, the Jewish Museum of Florida had bought the original 1929 synagogue building. They needed room to expand. The structures were restored yet again. In 2008, the museum connected the two buildings through a glass-domed structure. It was named after its donor: Bess Myerson. In 1945, she became the first—and remains the only—Jewish winner of the Miss America pageant. (More information about Meyerson can be found in chapter six.) The museum merged with Florida International University in 2012.

Tips for the Traveler: I recommend that you start your visit to the museum by looking at the timeline of Jewish history in Florida. It will show various events in historical perspective. Then venture into the permanent exhibit. Choose the themes you are interested in. They include politics, businesses, sports, religions, food, and much more. Take a look at the stained-glass window donated by and dedicated to Meyer Lansky, the organized crime mobster who was a member of the congregation.

Connecting the two buildings is Bessie's Bistro, donated by Miss America winner Bess Myerson. Though intended as a café, today it offers just a few self-service snacks. Pay upfront at the entrance.

The other building contains a rotating exhibit. Some displays feature unique photos you won't find elsewhere. A famous recent exhibit focused on the theme of Jewish food and restaurants.

Ask about tours of the museum from a volunteer docent. I highly recommend two walking tours, one of Jewish South Beach covering the area south of 5th Street and the other a Jewish food walking tour. The tours, led by Howard Brayer, are scheduled several times per month. Visit the museum website or call for his schedule. Customized tours are also offered to fit inflexible schedules.

The gift shop is also worth a look. Besides books and DVDs, the shop sells items like a ceramic Seder plate, pomegranate candlesticks, and decorative necklaces and pins.

The museum also hosts schools for educational exhibits and student workshops. If you're an educator, inquire about these programs.

But exhibits are only part of the offerings. The museum houses a vast collection of historical objects. Its website notes some of its significant holdings:

- Fannie Moss' Shell Apparel from a 1918 Jacksonville Young Men's Hebrew Association (YMHA) Purim party (a full dress, gloves, head covering and stockings made from Florida sea shells designed, sewn and worn by a Florida Jewish woman);
- Dzialynski Pocket Watch with hours in Hebrew with a bas-relief of Moses with the Ten Commandments on the reverse (the father of the watch's owner came to Jacksonville in 1850—the owner of the watch, George Dzialynski (1857-1937), was the first known Jewish boy born in Florida);
- Porcelain Plate from 1865 (owned by Henrietta Brash of Apalachicola) that was kashered in the Gulf of Mexico, demonstrating continuity of traditions;
- Confirmation Bible with ornate ivory and metal cover (printed in Vienna, 1911, presented to Ida Schwartz of Miami June 15, 1924);

- 19th Century Community Wedding Rings from central Europe traditionally worn by the bride at her wedding as well as the week following and then returned to the synagogue stewardship (Jacksonville family donated to collection);
- Hebrew/English citrus label used in an attempt to appeal to the Jewish market during the 1940s;
- Facsimile of the Rothschild Miscellany, originally printed in Italy in the 15th century. The Rothschild Miscellany is the "most elegantly and lavishly executed Hebrew manuscript of that era." It is regarded as "the most lavish Hebrew illuminated manuscript in existence."[5]

If you are a researcher or interested viewer, inquire about viewing any of these objects. Conversely, if you have an interesting photo or object to donate, the museum is actively seeking new items.

Finally, check the museum's website for evening activities like book talks, lectures, and other events.

Miami Design Preservation League
1001 Ocean Drive
Phone: (305) 672-2014
Website: https://www.mdpl.org
Hours: Tues.-Sun., 10 a.m.-5 p.m. (Thurs. until 7p.m.)

As you walk up the now posh Ocean Avenue, use your historic imagination. It did not always look the way it does now.

Chapter one of this book outlines the area's decline in the 1970s and 1980s. The sagging economy, rise in crime and drug trafficking, and decrease of tourism contributed to the decay. The Mariel boat lift in 1980 brought over many honorable Cuban refugees seeking freedom. But some were from Cuban jails and mental institutions. A significant portion of this sub-population settled in the Miami area, contributing to the crime increase.

Picture the bare streets that would have lay by the ocean during this era. Though plentiful today, cafes and restaurants were few. Tourists were scarce. Many residents were elderly Jews on fixed incomes. Some would sit on the porches of buildings, many of which had become rooming houses for residents. The neighborhood was dubbed "God's waiting room."

With a goal of capitalizing on the potential tourism, like their predecessors once had, developers expressed interest in tearing down old buildings for new structures. Historic architecture was in jeopardy.

Enter Barbara Capitman, a Jewish designer from New York who had moved to Miami in 1973. She and others appreciated the architecture of the past and started a movement that would preserve it at a time when few cared.

Specifically, Capitman saw how her copreservationists could color and enliven the neighborhood. This movement gave birth to the Miami Design Preservation League. Their first order of business was to conduct a survey of the buildings in South Beach.

Within a few years, their efforts bore fruit. In 1979, the Art Deco Historic District (formally called the Miami Beach Architectural District) was added to the National Register of Historic Places. This district encompasses most of South Beach—from 6th Street to 23rd Street, and from the beach to just two blocks east of Biscayne Bay, a total of about ten blocks east to west. The register prevents demolishing or significantly altering protected buildings' exteriors. Importantly, interiors can be changed. So can the use of the building.

The preservation efforts were successful in saving the buildings from demolition and in leading to an economic revitalization. Historic architecture was salvaged. Under the group's efforts, buildings were painted to be more colorful. This would ultimately catch the eye of movie producers and lead to South Beach as a key tourist destination.

Today, the Miami Design Preservation League's stated mission is to "preserve, protect and promote the cultural, social, economic, environmental and architectural integrity of the Miami Beach Architectural Historic District and all other areas of the City of Miami Beach where historic preservation is a concern."[6]

Tips for the Traveler: I recommend that you start off in the art deco welcome center. It's a small space that has brochures, local information, and guides to answer questions. Then enter the museum. It's very small and may take you about thirty minutes to an hour to go through, depending on your pace.

Read the information about the three major architectural designs: Mediterranean revival, art deco, and Miami modern (MiMo). The pictures and scale models on the wall illustrate them very well. Other mini-exhibits provide an overview of Miami Beach's development. In the center is a rotating exhibit. It tends to focus on trends, such as fashion. I recommend that you view at least part of the videos on the side to learn more about preservation efforts and the people behind them.

The center offers five different walking tours. I recommend you try at least one during your stay. They are on Jewish Miami Beach, the art deco movement, gay and lesbian life, and the MiMo architecture. Most are about $25 per person. Check the website for exact times.

The gift shop is also worth a visit. Check out some of the items for home décor.

I also recommend that you visit the league's website at http://www.mdpl.org/visual-memoirs-project/visual-memoirs-project to view recorded stories of Miami Beach residents. It will make your visit more personal. There's also an educational version aimed at middle-school students.

Wolfsonian Museum—FIU
1001 Washington Avenue
Phone: (305) 531-1001
Website: https://www.wolfsonian.org
Hours: Mon., Tue., Thu., Sat., 10 a.m.-6 p.m.; Wed., closed; Fri.,
10 a.m.-9 p.m. (free 6 p.m.-9 p.m.); Sun., noon-6 p.m.
Admission: $10 adults

As you walk north on Washington Avenue, you will come across
the Wolfsonian Museum. Like the Jewish Museum of Florida, the
Wolfsonian is part of the Florida International University.

It was named after Mitchell Wolfson Jr., a collector of
architecture and design memorabilia and a host of other objects.
Wolfson was born and raised in Miami Beach and is the son of
Miami Beach's first Jewish mayor, Mitchell Wolfson Sr.

His collection grew in the 1970s. In 1995, the museum opened
to the public. Two years later, Wolfson donated his collection
and museum facility to nearby Florida International University
(FIU). It was said to be the largest gift to a public university;
consequently, the museum became a division of FIU.

The museum houses a vast collection from the mid-nineteenth
century to the mid-twentieth century. Objects vary. Some are
glass, ceramic, or textile. The museum focuses on design and on
cultural expression through the display of objects. It conveys the
"persuasive power of art and design."[7]

Exhibit themes include Miami Beach's deco development,
Miami's skyscrapers, and Miami Beach classic hotels. Other
displays are structured around a movement. For example,
the museum hosted an exhibit called Women, Art and Social
Change that featured Newcomb Pottery. Another exhibit was a
photography display of World War I trenches. The museum tries
to shed light on cultural themes through its collection.

One angle consistent in its rotating exhibits is the role of pro-
paganda. An exhibit, for example, displayed political posters with
propagandistic messages from the Middle East and Afghanistan.

Smaller collections exist for British arts and crafts, Dutch art,
and world's fair posters.

> Tips for the Traveler: Some of the exhibits show clips from films from the 1940s or 1950s and are fun to watch.
>
> On Fridays from 6 p.m. to 9 p.m., admission is free. Guided tours are also offered at that time.
>
> The gift shop is worth a visit. It has a quaint café for the weary traveler or researcher.

World Erotic Art Museum
1205 Washington Avenue
Phone: (305) 532-9336
Website: https://weam.com
Hours: Mon.-Thurs., 11 a.m.-10 p.m.; Fri.-Sun., 11 a.m.-midnight
Admission: $15 adults

Think of it as the Metropolitan Museum of Art meets the Museum of Sex. This unique and risqué museum displays and explains a little discussed subject—the history of erotic art.

The collection is vast. It spans from ancient Egypt to Greece to the Americas and Asia. Some artists represented are household names like Picasso and Salvador Dali. Most are little known. Controversial artists like Robert Mapplethorpe are also displayed. The pieces vary from sculptures to tapestries and more.

The Jewish founder was Naomi Wilzig, whose husband, Siggi, was a Holocaust survivor liberated from Auschwitz. Many of the philanthropic Wilzig's causes were conventional, but because she wanted to exhibit the history of sexuality through art, she was dubbed the Queen of Erotic Art.

In 2005, Wilzig opened the doors to her museum. At the time, she explained that she "wanted to evoke the sensual experience of the pleasure and pain of love, and also wanted to send a message of tolerance in acknowledgement of the community and diversity of mankind."[8]

Wilzig intended to bring the museum's eclectic collections to Humboldt University of Berlin. Her act was, in a sense, meant to balance out history. The Nazis had stolen much from the collections from the Hirschfeld Institute, and she hoped to rectify such theft. However, Wilzig would not live to see that wish realized. She died in 2014.

Tips for the Traveler: The museum will not admit anyone under the age of eighteen. It is open late, so if your schedule during the day is tight, leave this one for the evening.

As you enter the exhibit, you will visit a series of rooms. By the end of the hallway, you will be back at the main entrance.

I recommend you survey rooms from different periods and cultures. Beyond its erotic subject matter, that is what makes the art unique. Collections include pieces related to Greek and Roman mythology, Asian art (from China, Japan, or India), ethnographic African art, and pre-Columbian and folk art.

Be sure to find the chair associated with Catherine the Great. The art of movie stars and pin-up girls are interesting to view as well. They feature Marilyn Monroe, Betty Page, and more.

Above all, keep an open mind and enjoy the exhibits.

Notable Hotels

Fashionhaus Hotel, now Fashion Boutique Hotel
534 Washington Avenue
Phone: (786) 398-4408
Website: www.fashionboutiquehotel.com

If you're interested in studying key architects in Miami Beach and their notable projects, take a look at the Fashionhaus Hotel. It was built in 1939 by Henry Hohauser as the Henry Hotel, modestly named after the architect. Hohauser and his wife, who lived further north in Miami Beach, would stay here.

Henry Hohauser was one of the fathers of the art deco movement in the 1930s. His style is most noted for its "streamlined curves, jutting towers, window 'eyebrows,' and neon."[9] His style was less ornate, and his buildings cost less to construct. His customers tended to be middle-class vacationers rather than those seeking luxury and opulence.

Decades later, some of his buildings fell out of style, considered drab. Historical preservationists like Barbara Capitman and

Leonard Horowitz reinvigorated this movement in the late 1970s and 1980s. (To learn more about Henry Hohauser, view the show on him on PBS's renowned series *American Experience*.)

His projects were extensive and included synagogues, apartment buildings, and hotels. Here is a partial list of properties in Miami Beach that Hohauser worked on:

1600 Michigan Avenue (1936)
1610 Pennsylvania Avenue (1937)
6971 Carlyle Avenue (1947)
The Aloha–1457 Meridian Avenue (1937)
The Beth Jacob Synagogue–301 Washington Avenue (1936 building only)
The Cardozo Hotel–1300 Ocean Drive (1939)
The Chelsea–530 15th Street (1938)
Collins Park–318 20th Street (1939)
The Colony Hotel–736 Ocean Drive (1935)
Crescent Hotel–1420 Ocean Drive (1938)
Dolphin Hotel Apartments–8400 Harding Avenue (1949)
Edison Hotel–960 Ocean Drive (1935)
Essex House Hotel–1001 Collins Avenue (1938)
The Helene Marie–1050 Jefferson Avenue (1939)
Jerry's Deli (Hoffman's Cafeteria)–1450 Collins Ave (1940)
The Mansfield Park–1925 Washington Avenue (1949)
Parc Vendome–736 13th Street (1936)
The Park Central Hotel–640 Ocean Drive (1937)
The Vintage East–1250 Drexel Avenue (1939)
The Webster Hotel–1220 Collins Avenue (1939)
The White Apartments–405 76th Street[10]

Lord Balfour Hotel

350 Ocean Drive
Phone: (305) 673-0401
Website: https://room-matehotels.com

Walking along Ocean Drive, you'll come across a yellow art deco building behind palm trees with the lettering "Lord Balfour." It is named after Arthur Lord Balfour, the British prime minister and later foreign minister. Opened in 1940, its aesthetic is quintessentially art deco.

Why did the owner choose Balfour as the hotel's namesake? Because the owner of the hotel admired him. In particular, the owner appreciated Balfour's support for a Jewish homeland in Palestine, which was publicized in 1917 in his famed Balfour Declaration. The declaration was actually a letter from Balfour to Lord Rothschild that "led the League of Nations to entrust the United Kingdom with the Palestine Mandate in 1922."[11]

Observe the exterior's art deco elements. Then enter the hotel lobby if you can. Much of the interior has been modernized. An original feature is the terrazzo floor, a very common floor material in art deco buildings in the area.

Another original feature is the elevator door. Walk around the concierge desk and you will find a relic from the past, something that those who grew up with mobile phones likely know nothing about—the hotel's original switchboard!

A *New York Times* review describes the lobby eloquently. "The hotel eschews trite English décor—club chairs, wood paneling—for brash, colorful, contemporary spaces enlivened by playful details. The lobby sets the tone."[12]

Finally, look up. Read the quotes on the ceiling from Lord Balfour and Winston Churchill. One proclaims, "History does not repeat itself. Historians repeat each other."

Nemo (Prime) Hotel
100 Ocean Drive
Phone: (305) 532-0553
Website: http://www.primehotelmiami.com

Nemo Hotel was the first kosher hotel in Miami Beach. Built in 1921 by Joseph and Harry Goodkowsky of Maine and Sam Magid of Boston, it catered to Jews at a time few other institutions would. The hotel was fashionable during the 1940s as soldiers came to town for training.

Harry's daughter, Myra Far, illustrates the carefree environment at the hotel's start. "We frolicked on the beach at 10th Street, met all the boys, ordered corned beef sandwiches, ate ice cream at Dolly Madison's. We even watched the turtles lay eggs."

Myra tells of "the 'politically incorrect' Workmen's Circle Jews, who would get into trouble for their views." They would "hang out at the beach to play lotto and bingo or entertain each other with labor songs."[13]

But starting in the 1950s and into the 1960s, the once lively hotel fell into disrepair. A former Miami Beach city commissioner called the entire area a "disaster." He wistfully recalled, "Many of the hotels had fallen into disrepair. The old hoteliers had mortgages they couldn't pay, and no bank would help them. Then in the '70s young people started coming down, and New Yorkers made real estate investments, buying up three and four hotels at once."[14]

In the 1990s, the Nemo Hotel was purchased by an enterprising restauranteur. The interior has changed, but the black and white tile floor is original. It became the Nemo Restaurant.

But it did not last. In 2011, the acclaimed eatery closed. The Prime Fish from restauranteur Myles Chefetz replaced it.

The architecture is Mediterranean revival, which was popular in Miami Beach during the hotel's heyday in the 1920s and 1930s.

Some typical features of the style that are seen in the Nemo are arched windows or doorways and a stucco facade. Another common feature, which can be seen in part of the courtyard area, is a barrel tile roof.

Beyond the building, take a look at the large tree in the courtyard. It is a one hundred year old pigeon plum tree. Unlike many planted trees, it is native to the area.

Park Central Hotel
640 Ocean Drive
Phone: (305) 538-1611
Website: https://theparkcental.com

Observe this art deco hotel designed by Henry Hohauser in 1937. You may not realize by looking at it but it represents a major architecture revitalization effort from the 1980s. The property was bought and renovated by businessman Tony Goldman. The effort brought investor confidence to the then-fledgling area.

Aesthetically, the building showcases the great efforts of a little-known Jewish preservationist, Leonard Horowitz. One of the original leaders of the preservation movement, Horowitz created a palette of colors for art deco buildings to accentuate the architectural details. Most buildings had drab neutral colors. Horowitz envisioned light pastel colors to enliven the area—and the mood.

Horowitz emulated nature in his color palette selection. The colors of the sky and sea were used.

The world took notice. Miami Beach began to be recognized for its pastel colors. The hit TV show from the 1980s, *Miami Vice*, used some of these buildings for its set.

Park Central is one of few buildings still standing that Horowitz designed the colors for. Another is the Winter Haven Hotel at 14th and Ocean.

Former Sites of Famous Places

The places discussed in this section sadly are no longer there. Still, you can visit the sites on which they once existed and read about their unfamiliar stories.

Site of Bernstein's Jewish Home Cooking
Southwest intersection of 1st and Ocean

Bernstein's may have been the first Jewish-style restaurant in Miami Beach. It was owned and operated by Esther and Oscar Bernstein and their daughters, Rose and Eva. The Bernsteins moved to Miami Beach in 1927.

Prior to World War II, not all establishments offered printed menus. Offerings were more limited than in contemporary restaurants and dependent on what was fresh and available. Signs out front might have showcased what was available.

The sign in front of Bernstein's, though, was more general. It read "Jewish Home Cooking. Sandwiches. Regular Dinners. A la carte. Charcoal Steak." On the top, the sign added, "Soups of All Kinds."

Site of Hebrew Home of South Beach
336 Collins Avenue

This site at 336 Collins was originally the Lido Hotel, built in 1935. Around this time, the region was recovering from the depression and the devastating hurricane of 1926.

The site then became the Hebrew Home of South Beach, a 104-bed assisted living facility. It was founded by twelve Jewish women in 1954 specifically for elderly Jewish people and Jewish war veterans.

Eventually, it became part of the non-profit Plaza Health Network, which runs nursing homes across Miami-Dade County. The facility became open to all.

In 2013, however, it closed its doors. Residents were dispersed among the other Plaza Health Network facilities. The move was controversial as employees were laid off on the key holiday of Yom Kippur.

The organization was also named in a whistleblower's lawsuit filed in Miami Federal Court by an ex-finance executive. The suit claims that the real estate developer devised a plan to "dole out secret kickbacks to dozens of south Florida physicians who referred hundreds of Medicaid and Medicare patients to Plaza Health's eight nursing and rehabilitation centers."[15] Essentially, the suit claimed that Plaza falsified services performed in order to scam Medicare and Medicaid.

In 2015, the Hebrew Homes Network, Inc. paid $17 million to settle the case. The whistleblower received a quarter of that.

The building will become a hotel and a condo, but a portion of the property may remain untouched as it is considered a historic structure.

Site of the Home of Henry Levi
1030 Washington Avenue

This house belonged to the French Jewish immigrant Henry Levi. He was one of the few Jews who was able to live above the informal border of 5th Street during Miami Beach's early days. He was one of the key builders of the area in the 1920s.

In his earlier career, Levi built a movie theater chain. After *Birth of a Nation*, silent movies proliferated. Several years later, he moved to Miami Beach to undergo a laborious task: to create an island from naturally swampy land in Biscayne Bay. In 1926, the work began. He and his crew underwent a two-year, twenty-four-hour-a-day dredging to form what would become Normandy Isle in the northern part of Miami Beach. Fittingly, the streets have French names: Beatriz Court, Marseille Drive, and

Normandy Court. In the 1930s, he also built the town of Surfside.
The building is among the oldest in Miami Beach. Erected in
1922, it was made of a material that was plentiful, functional, and
aesthetic at the time: limestone.

Site of Home of Rose Weiss
221 Collins Avenue

Unrelated to the Weiss family from Joe's Stone Crab, who were the
first permanent Jewish settlers of Miami Beach, Rose Weiss and
her husband, Jeremiah, moved into this house in 1920 and were
the second permanent Jewish residents. Like the other Weisses,
Rose Weiss, Jeremiah, and their children moved from New York
due to health issues related to asthma.

Rose Weiss would become a prominent figure in the budding
community. She was known as "the mother of Miami Beach." A
devoted citizen, she attended nearly every city council meeting for
almost four decades. In 1950, she designed the official flag of Miami
Beach, which featured bright green and gold with a seal and a palm
tree. She suggested the city's slogan, Forward with Caution.

Her volunteer work extended into city administration. She served
as head of the city's welfare department. Also, during the war bond
campaign of World War II, she outsold all women in Florida.

In 1975, the city passed a resolution for Rose Weiss Park to be
a public space at the corner of Washington Avenue and 2nd Street
near the home she once lived in. It does not appear, however, that
the park is still named for her. (See chapter six to learn more about
Rose Weiss.)

Site of Jean's Candy Shop
212 Collins Avenue

Across the street from Rose Weiss's home was Jean's Candy
Shop. Jewish owned, it operated in the 1930s and 1940s. Later, it
relocated to the pedestrian mall of Lincoln Road.

Some vintage pictures of Jean's Candy Shop showcase Miami
Beach's important role as an army training center during the
1940s. In one picture, soldiers gather around the shop. Perhaps
they had a sweet tooth.

Jean Candy Shop at 212 Collins Avenue in 1939. (From the collections of the Jewish Museum of Florida-FIU, originated by Marcia Jo Zerivitz, founding executive director.)

Site of Al's Restaurant

On this site was a well-known restaurant and all-night cafeteria.

On Thanksgiving Day 1934, Abraham Al Galbut and his wife, Bessie, arrived in Miami Beach. It was starting to recover from its economic depression and the destructive hurricane just eight years prior. Opportunity abounded.

The young Jewish entrepreneurial couple would soon own several businesses on the corner of 5th Street and Washington Avenue. A newsstand, auto tag agency, travel agency, and driving school were among these varied establishments.

Bessie was very active in setting up Jewish cultural and philanthropic causes on the new island. The Jewish Community Center was named for the Galbut family, as was the Bessie Galbut Daughters of Israel Mikvah Center (ritual bath).

Ultimately, the Galbut family became one of the best-known Miami Beach families.

Site of Blackstone Hotel

Look north on Washington Avenue at the large tan building on the west side of the street. This was the first hotel north of 5th Street to allow Jewish guests. According to some reports, this was the site where George Gershwin wrote parts of his groundbreaking *Porgy and Bess*. He composed the opera, which included a libretto written by his brother Ira Gershwin and Dubose Heyward, in 1934. It was based on Heyward's novel and play, which were both titled *Porgy*. Unusual in the mid-1930s, the cast were African American singers. Gershwin referred to it as a folk opera. It depicts a disabled and indigent beggar living in the slums of Charleston, South Carolina, who attempts to save Bess from her dangerous and bad-tempered lover.

Just as the opera was groundbreaking for 1935, the hotel in which it was written would be revolutionary three decades later. In 1954, the Blackstone became one of the first hotels in Miami Beach to allow black guests.

Site of Famous Restaurant
671 Washington Avenue

Famous Restaurant represented a time when delis were popular and patrons looked forward to free coleslaw and pickles. The restaurant went out of business a few decades ago, but it has an interesting culinary past.

Famous was opened in 1945 by Morris Lerner and operated as the Famous until 1981. Patrons looked forward to the ritual of coleslaw, pickles, sauerkraut, and several kinds of bread on their table. Bottles of seltzer were complimentary, a rarity today. Sometimes, the innovative patron requested chocolate syrup to mix with the seltzer to make a chocolate soda.

The menu included the usual list of items for a deli in the Eastern European style: matzoh ball soup, stuffed kishka (beef intestine stuffed with a mixture of flour or matzoh meal, chicken fat, and spices), boiled beef flanken (short ribs), and brisket of beef.

Then, in the late 1970s, customer tastes changed. To win customers back, the restaurant placed ads in the local newspaper noting that portions were smaller. The restaurant management realized that smaller was "in." But the restaurant was never able to regain lost customers and acquire new ones in the numbers they would need.

Other well-known Miami Beach delis included Wolfie's (21st Street and Collins, and also at Lincoln Road and Collins) and Pumpernick's (67th Street and Collins). Sadly, all of these are now closed.

Site of Friedman's Bakery

On the corner of 7th Street and Washington Avenue—at the current location of Manolo Restaurant—was the famed Friedman's Kosher Bakery. The sign used to read "Fresh Baking All Day— Bread, Challahs, Rolls, Cakes." The top of the sign resembled a festive cake with icing, and its lettering was partially painted in a stark blue and red.

This was the first building in South Beach that Leonard Horowitz painted to revitalize the drab looking buildings.

Site of 5th Street Gym
555 Washington Avenue

On this site was the 5th Street Gym, opened in 1950 by Chris and Angelo Dundee. Most notably, it served as Muhammed Ali's training site.

A less prominent figure is associated with the gym. Benjamin "Evil Eye" Finkle was infamous for his "Evil Eye hex." In the mid-1920s, former boxer Finkle informed sports writers that his right eye had "evil powers." Elite athletes took notice. In time, famed trainers called upon Finkle's supernatural services to sway the outcome of games. Notable clients include Jack Dempsey and Sugar Ray Robinson. Finkle's services were not cheap; he charged between $50 and $300 (in 1930s dollars) to influence boxing matches with his eye. Dan Parker, a New York sports columnist, dubbed Finkle the number-one hex-man in the world.

Finkle's interests were apparently not limited to boxing and sports fixing. He seemed interested in fashion and reportedly owned fifty-nine pairs of shoes.

The original gym closed in 1994. It reopened in the current building in 2010 but closed just three years later. Today, it is located on Alton Road, about one mile north.

Other Notable Sites

Versace's House
1116 Ocean Drive

Many visitors to Miami Beach are curious about the house of Italian fashion icon Gianni Versace. This magnificent house right on Ocean Drive was built in 1930. Miami Beach was recovering from the damaging hurricane of 1926. The Mediterranean revival style was prominent at the time.

Originally a single-family home, it was converted into an apartment house in 1937 called the Amsterdam Place.

In 1992, Gianni Versace purchased it. The building once again became a single-family home. The fashion guru completely

Versace's mansion on Ocean Drive. Today, it is a restaurant. (Photo by Aaron Davidson.)

redecorated it. He had headline-grabbing guests. Sadly, he would only live there for five years. In July 1997, Andrew Cunanan killed Versace right in front of his house.

Today, the mansion is a hotel and restaurant. Visitors can see the inside only by patronizing the restaurant.

In some way, Versace's legacy may live through the hotel. It is extravagant over-the-top luxury. "The mansion features a 54-foot mosaic-tiled swimming pool lined in 24-carat gold, an original feature designed by Versace. According to the website, all bedrooms, outfitted in Egyptian cotton linens, have their own private balcony or patio and luxurious Italian marble bathrooms."[16]

Historic Eateries

Joe's Stone Crab Restaurant
11 Washington Avenue
Phone: (305) 673-0365
Website: https://www.joesstonecrab.com

Joe's Stone Crab Restaurant dates back to Miami Beach's original development. It is the oldest and arguably most famous restaurant in Miami Beach.

Joe and Jennie Weiss left Hungary for New York. They both worked in the restaurant business, Joe as a waiter and Jennie as a cook. Yet Joe's health problems would upend their plans to live in the bustling metropolis. After diagnosing Joe with severe asthma, a doctor explained that his only cure would be to move to a favorable climate.

The Weisses' son Jesse recounted the move: "My dad borrowed $50 on his life insurance policy, left my mother and me in New York and came to Florida. He stayed in Miami one night, and he couldn't breathe. So he took the ferry boat that used to go to Miami Beach. Oddly enough, he could breathe there."[17]

Led by his ailment, Joe's timing was impeccable for business opportunities in the nascent city of Miami Beach. Prior to any bridge built from Miami, visitors came to Miami Beach for a day-trip of swimming and card playing. Casinos, which did not offer games of chance, provided swimming, changing rooms, and eateries.

Weiss set out to convince the owner of Smith's Casino, Avery Smith, of his cooking talents. He sold not only his culinary skills

The iconic Joe's Stone Crab Restaurant in the 1930s, one of the oldest restaurants in the area. (From the collections of the Jewish Museum of Florida-FIU, originated by Marcia Jo Zerivitz, founding executive director.)

but his ability to promote the casino. He said he could bring in more patronage. Defending from competition from other casinos, Avery Smith decided to take a chance on the unknown cook.

It was in Smith's bathing casino that the Weisses' culinary career was launched. They opened a lunch counter where guests could buy fish sandwiches and fries. It was sea fare but nothing like what they would one day be famous for.

Joe's granddaughter describes the scene: "You'd come over and rent lockers to change your clothes to use the ocean or use the pool. The women used to have the long bathing suits with the stockings . . . that was 1913. Collins Avenue was not really a street—it was sort of a trail with ruts in it. In 1918, Joe and Jennie bought a bungalow near the casino, on Biscayne Street. They moved into the back, set up seven or eight tables on the front porch, cooked in the kitchen, and called it Joe's Restaurant."[18]

The new entrepreneurs reprised their roles as cook and waiter. But this time they owned their restaurant. Some of the food served included mackerel, pompano, and snapper. Absent were the namesake stone crabs. The restaurant enjoyed being one of the only ones on the newly emerging beach; competition was scarce.

According to restaurant stories, Jennie decided which customers could be served. If she felt a man was with his mistress, for example, she would refuse service. Yet she seemed to have a soft spot for the mob. Al Capone, for example, was welcome, usually under the alias Al Brown. He preferred to dine early. Jennie is reported to have one day encountered the famed gangster, saying, "Mr. Brown, I must tell you something. If I don't like somebody, I don't allow them to come in here, but you've always been a gentleman, and anytime you want to come into this restaurant, you can."[19]

On Mother's Day each year, Jennie received flowers with the mysterious message, "Good luck Mother Joe's." The giver of the present remains unknown. Some thought it was their loyal patron Al Capone.

Three years after opening the restaurant, Joe and Jennie's culinary offerings turned a corner. At this time, no one knew how to eat stone crabs, much less though of doing so.

Joe was slow to warm to the idea. While stone crabs were plentiful in the surrounding waters, he did not think patrons would eat them. But this would soon change. Arriving with a bag of live stone crabs, Joe and an oceanic researcher experimented with how to cook them. Before long, stone crabs made their way to the top of the menu, usually served with brown potatoes, coleslaw, and mayonnaise. Patrons loved them. They paid $0.75 for four. Jessie Weiss noted, "We hit the jackpot with that one!"[20]

The restaurant itself was a destination. Frequented by Hollywood stars, mobsters, politicians, and famous journalists, it was a place to be seen. Stars included Will Rogers, Amelia Earhart, the Duke and Duchess of Windsor, and J. Edgar Hoover.

In subsequent decades, the restaurant thrived despite the hurricane, increased competition, economic depressions, and other major changes. In the 1970s and 1980s, the restaurant's neighborhood was known as one of high crime and drug trafficking. Yet Joe's persevered through multiple generations of the Weiss family.

In 1940, Damon Runyon produced a satirical essay called "The Brighter Side" that lamented the popularity of eating stone crab. He writes, "One of the more regrettable circumstances attendant upon the tourist invasion of Dade County, Florida of recent winters was the discovery by visitors of the stone crab. The home folks . . . can remember when they were so numerous that a man could dip a foot anywhere in Biscayne Bay and come up with a stone crab hanging on each toe. However, now they are scarce and costly."[21] Look for the postcard at the restaurant.

Comparison of prices in 1963 to today:

Clam chowder: $0.50/$6.95
Stone crabs: $3.25/$50.00 (approximate cost depending on size)
Ice cream: $0.40/$5.25

Total: $4.15/$62.20

Tips for the Traveler: Today, the restaurant serves meals throughout the day. During dinner, there is the informal section with self-service and the formal dining area. If possible, try formal dining for the full experience.

In the rear hallway, look at the historic photos. One is of the Biscayne Bay and Smith's Casino, where the founder once worked. Look also for the photo of the opening of the Collins Bridge across the Biscayne Bay. Another photo has a sign proclaiming the construction of a new pier: "This is the island of fairy land. It is the private property of the Biscayne Navigation Company." It notes that others will be charged a $0.25 admission fee.

For ordering, I recommend the classic combination of the namesake stone crab or crab cake combined with the famous coleslaw (shredded cabbage, sweet cider vinegar, tomatoes, mayonnaise, and sweet relish). It comes with hash browns, creamed spinach, and a slice of key lime pie.

If you are just ordering dessert, I strongly recommend the key lime pie. It is considered one of the best in the area. You should not leave Florida without trying key lime pie somewhere, if not here.

If you want a sandwich, consider the lobster role or the lobster reuben, a lesser-known dish that combines a deli style sandwich with seafood.

Another recommendation, if you're interested in sampling different kinds of seafood, is the cold seafood platter. This display includes stone crabs, shrimp, oysters, and half of a Florida lobster.

Prime 112 Restaurant (formerly Browns Hotel)
112 Ocean Drive
Phone: (305) 532-8112
Website: http://mylesrestaurantgroup.com

As you walk along 1st Street and Ocean Drive, you will see the site of Miami Beach's oldest existing building and its first hotel, built in 1915. Look for the brown lettering of the sign Browns Hotel above the yellow doorway. The original name was the Atlantic Beach Hotel. It harkens back to a time when many Miami Beach residents did not allow Jewish clientele. For the first several decades of Miami Beach's development, many hotels restricted clientele. In fact, they often used that exact phrasing in advertising: restricted clientele. Some were explicit, utilizing the phrase "gentiles only." So this hotel was frequented by Jews and others who were denied entrance elsewhere.

The architecture is vernacular, which was popular in Miami Beach's early days of the 1910s and 1920s. The building itself is composed of local materials. It showcases that which was plentiful in this period—namely, limestone. That is used here in the short wall along the sidewalk.

With the neighborhood's steep decline in the 1970s and 1980s, this area was a center for drug activity and crime. Today, that is unnoticeable. Quite the contrary, it is now an upscale steak restaurant called Prime 112.

Prime 112 is one of several local restaurants owned by Myles Chefetz. He also owns Prime Italian, Prime Fish, and Big Pink (see page 77). Chefetz is a former New York lawyer who was ready for a career change. On vacation in 1994, he realized the opportunity to enhance restaurants in Miami Beach. Then, restaurants were "club-like environments where each attracted customers on specific nights of the week." Chefetz decided to offer a different experience. The restaurant claims that he is unofficially the "Sultan of South of Fifth."[22]

Next to Prime 112, you will see the boutique and high-end Prime Hotel. Go inside and ask if you may look at the pictures of old Miami Beach.

Well-known Eateries

Big Pink
157 Collins Avenue
Phone: (305) 532-4700
Website: http://mylesrestaurantgroup.com

Myles Chefetz also opened the aptly named Big Pink. The large pink exterior creates a retro diner experience. Think huge menus, stainless steel trays, breakfast food served all day, and late-night hours. The décor is also retro. Note the pink Volkswagen Beetles and TVs lining the wall. It's like a diner of yesterday meets an art gallery. The food selection is vast.

Babylon Turkish Restaurant
560 Washington Avenue
Phone: (786) 216-7230
Website: http://babylonmiamibeach.com

Babylon features a very friendly, laid-back atmosphere right off highly trafficked Washington Avenue and 5th Street. Try the signature Turkish breakfasts. In the evenings, ask about the live music and belly dancing shows. The décor inside is also noteworthy. Many displayed objects have significance in Turkish culture. Food-wise, there are Turkish signature dishes as well as Greek, Israeli, and Kosher options.

   If possible, ask for a table on the patio. You'll be transported from the hustle and bustle of South Beach and might even feel like you're in Istanbul.

My Ceviche
1250 South Miami Avenue
Phone: (305) 960-7825
Website: http://www.myceviche.com

This small, take-out only Mexican shop was started by Sam Gorenstein, a Jewish chef formerly with BLT Steak on South Beach, and his partner, Roger Duarte of George Stone Crab. It's best known for its ceviche, which is served with the signature combination of red onions, cilantro, jalapenos, tomatoes, sweet potato, and yellow corn. You can choose flavors like Aji Amarillo, which contains lime juice, lemon juice, orange juice, Aji Amarillo, and ginger. Or try the usual fare of burritos, tacos, or stone crabs. True to Miami Beach, it sells key lime pie too.

Pita Loca
601 Collins Avenue, Ste. 5
Phone: (305) 673-3388
Website: http://www.pitaloca.com

Think of it as a kosher pita place meets the beach. Literally steps from Ocean Drive, Pita Loca serves Israeli and Middle Eastern cuisine like falafel, kebabs, dips, and salads. It's very casual, and the meats are "Glatt Kosher."

Fish are imported in the quick-service restaurant and then prepared on the premises.

Miami Beach Jewish Sites (between 12th Street and 40th Street)

Sites of Famous Places

Cinema Theater (now Mansion)
1235 Washington Avenue

Like many former Yiddish theaters in New York, this building served many functions over the decades. Opened in 1934 as a nightclub, a few years later, it transitioned to a movie theater under the auspices of the Florida State Theater chain. The auditorium was colored in red with large murals hanging by sofas. By the 1950s, double features were the rage. The cinema played MGM double feature films like *Bride of the Gorilla*.

Later, it was converted into a Yiddish Theater. The entertainment tended to be more variety/vaudeville style rather than one-story dramas or comedies. As Yiddish theater waned in popularity, the building changed once again. It reverted to its original function as a night club. The famed rock 'n' roll musician Prince owned the club at one point. Yiddish Theater, Prince, and a nightclub: an interesting combination.

From 2004 until 2015, it was the home of the Mansion nightclub.

Yet in late 2015 the club closed. It reopened in 2016 under a new name, concept, and management. The new name, Icon, harkens back to the venue's days as a theater. It's now a thirty-thousand-square-foot, art-deco inspired space. It uses technology to create a multi-sensory experience.

Wolfie's Delicatessen
17190 Collins Avenue

One of the locations of the famed Wolfie's Delicatessen was on this site. The classic old-time Jewish deli was started by Wilfred Cohen. The other was on Collins at 21st Street. Once a busboy at a Catskills, Pennsylvania, restaurant, Cohen traveled to Miami Beach around 1940 and purchased Al's Sandwich Shop. He expanded it.

After World War II, the influx of tourists and residents alike flocked to Wolfie's. Some residents in kitchen-less rooming houses also frequented it. Advertisers took notice. In 1959, the now defunct Northeast Airlines selected Wolfie's to cater meals to passengers flying from Miami to New York.

Cohen also owned Pumpernik's on Collins, as well as Rascal House on 172nd Street in northern Miami Beach.

Old-timers recall the "baskets of assorted varieties of miniature rolls and Danishes and stainless steel buckets of pickles, sauerkraut, and other vegetables served at no additional cost with meals."[23]

Sadly, all of them are now closed.

Pedestrian Destinations

Espanola Way

Stroll down a Spanish village . . . in Miami Beach.

Envisioned by N. B. T. Roney in 1925 as the "historic Spanish village," the small pedestrian way was modeled after Mediterranean towns. Spanish colonial architecture predominates. Espanola Way is just two blocks, but it is worth a visit for its restaurants and shopping. It's off the more trafficked streets. Look at the windows and door arches; observe the potted plants along the sidewalk.

Take a break from your sightseeing, enjoy the ocean breeze, and sip a cocktail or coffee.

Lincoln Road

Only about a century ago, Lincoln Road was a forest of mangroves. In 1912, developer Carl Fisher saw the island as a playground for the affluent, the 5th Avenue of the South. He hired laborers to tirelessly clear a strip to become the town's early social center. Lincoln Road was at the center of the newly developed island. Fisher's office was located on the newly paved Lincoln Road.

By the late 1950s, Lincoln Road became a destination. Whereas most areas of the United States were making way for the car, this road took the opposite path. It became a pedestrian-only street. As art deco gave way to the then-popular Miami modern architecture (or MiMo), gardens, theaters, restaurants, and hotels were built. Shopping was moving to other parts of Miami Beach, so this development brought some of it back to Lincoln Road.

Yet, in the 1960s and 1970s, empty storefronts lined the once-popular road. By the late 1980s and 1990s, the road became yet again a key tourist destination, only to once more fall into disrepair by 1997. A major restoration was in place particularly for worn fountains and gardens.

The subsequent decades saw its revival. Today, it is a top destination for tourists and some locals for shopping, dining, or people-watching.

Tips for the Traveler: Stroll down Lincoln Road and take in the environment. I recommend Books & Books to browse. It is one of the largest independent bookstores in the US. The store carries some unique books on the area and much more.

Pay a visit to the newly restored Colony Theater, a noted performing arts venue. Or visit the ArtsCenter of South Florida and browse paintings and sculptures from local artists.

Here are places of Jewish interest along Lincoln Road to visit:

Temple House
1415 Euclid Avenue
Phone: (305) 673-2526
Website: www.thetemplehouse.com

In 1933, noted architect L. Murray Dixon built this large, two-story, single family residence. He would go on to build famed art deco buildings like the Victor Hotel.

A decade later, the huge home would be converted to the Joseph-Jacob Congregation. Later, it was expanded and housed the Orthodox Knesseth Israel.

In 2003, it returned to a single-family house. The present owner is Daniel Davidson. Temple House may be the largest single-family residence in South Beach. Celebrities including Magic Johnson, Venus Williams, and Al Gore drop in for parties.

Frieze Ice Cream Factory
1626 N Michigan Avenue
Phone: (786) 502-9236

Just off Lincoln Road is the Frieze Ice Cream Factory. Try some of the ice cream and non-dairy sorbets. Some recommend the watermelon, champagne, or lychee sorbet flavors. The ice cream and sorbets are kosher.

Chabad of Lincoln Road
669 Lincoln Lane North
Phone: (305) 242-2231
Website: mbjewish.com

Found throughout Miami Beach—or around the globe, for that matter—Chabad Houses are run by members of the Lubavitch movement. The houses offer classes, prayer services, holiday celebrations, and additional innovative programming.

Historic Synagogues

Temple Beth Shmuel-the Cuban Hebrew Congregation
1719 Michigan Avenue
Phone: (305) 604-9101
Website: www.cubanhebrew.com

Located just a block from the famous Lincoln Road, the Conservative, Ashkenazi Cuban Hebrew Congregation of Miami has a unique story. It's about the Jewish-Cuban refugees fleeing to Florida and finding a home and community.

In September 1961, the Cuban Hebrew Circle of Miami was adopted in the Lucerne Hotel. Thirteen enterprising members were present. Within two years, the new group rented a place to meet at 1534 Washington Avenue. After a series of moves to nearby locations, in 1965 the budding congregation changed its name to the Cuban Hebrew Congregation.

The congregation took on more than religious functions. It advocated for and helped settle Cuban refugees. Significantly, it

Temple Beth Shmuel-the Cuban Hebrew Congregation played a large role in welcoming Cuban Jews during the 1960s. (Photo by Aaron Davidson.)

hosted a table at Opa-Locka Airport to greet refugees arriving from Cuba and aided Cubans wanting to come to South Florida through the Freedom Flights.

In the 1970s, the congregation conceived the El Nuevo Casino for members to socialize. By 1975, the small synagogue building opened on this site on Michigan Avenue.

Soon, the congregation incorporated Cuban relics into rituals. In 1980, services were conducted with a one-hundred-year-old Torah, prayer cap, and tallit from El Patronato in Havana.

In the early 1980s, another wave of Cuban refugees came to Miami Beach through the Mariel boat lifts. The congregation responded in kind.

The larger building, currently used by the congregation, opened in 1984. It also has a Montessori School.

Currently, the number of Cuban Jewish households in Miami is estimated at about twenty-five hundred, though the number changes based upon definitions used.

Tips for the Traveler: The outside is worth a look. Note the globe design on the front doors. If you are able to attend an event or service, you can see the pretty interior of the sanctuary. The temple showcases ornate stained glass windows of the Twelve Tribes of Israel. Note the candelabras next to the bimah; they were created by Mexican artist Naomi Siegman.

Also, look for interesting programs open to the public. For example, the congregation hosted a program called the Jewish Community of Cuba: An Overview.

Temple Emanu-El
1701 Washington Avenue
Phone: (305) 538-2503
Website: www.tesobe.org

Walking up Washington Avenue, you will come upon the oldest Conservative congregation in Miami Beach. The sanctuary is among the most beautiful. Its interior of Byzantine and Moorish architecture has a colorful, cool Mediterranean feel. The imposing blue rotunda roof stands about ten stories tall.

The building's storied past begins in 1938 with the newly

formed Congregation Jacob Joseph of Miami Beach. In 1940, the congregation grew to two hundred members, each of whom gave $10 in yearly dues. The Orthodox congregation became the Miami Beach Community Jewish Center and subsequently the Miami Beach Jewish Center.

In time, the congregation split into the Orthodox and Conservative groups. After World War II, the Miami Beach Jewish Center opened a new building modeled after the Great Synagogue in Oran, Algeria. By the 1950s, the now Conservative congregation changed its name yet again. It became Temple Emanu-El, meaning "May God be with us."

During this period, civil rights protests gripped the south. Rabbi Lehrman advocated for civil rights and for ending segregation in the South.

The congregation expanded in 1966 with Morris Lapidus, the famed designer of the Fontainebleau Hotel, supervising its construction.

In subsequent decades, the congregation thrived. Rabbi Lehrman published a book in 1979, *The Name of God.*

In the 1980s, as Cuban refugees came to South Beach, the temple was challenged to adjust its programming to reflect the needs of Cuban Jews.

By 1992, Rabbi Lehrman retired after almost fifty years of service. In the early 2000s, Phillip Frost funded a thorough renovation of the sanctuary for $2 million. The new Frost Sanctuary emerged. In 2010, two decorative pieces were added to the Temple: a "Dove of Peace" designed by Kenneth Treister and a Jerusalem stone were added to the main entrance and nearby plaza.

Guests of the temple read like a Who's Who of international leaders, including former president Bill Clinton, the Dalai Lama, and South Africa's Desmond Tutu.

Tips for the Traveler: Temple Emanu-El is now offering
tours. They are scheduled every Monday and Wednesday at
1:30 p.m. The cost is $5, and they last thirty minutes.
   The sanctuary is one of a kind. You may think you are
in southern Europe or the Middle East as you gaze at the
Moorish architecture and many colors. The twelve tribes of
Israel are represented near the bimah. Try to see this one-
of-a-kind sanctuary on a tour. Notice also the pictures of
graduating classes from the late 1940s to more recent years.

Memorials

Holocaust Beach
1933-1945 Meridian Avenue
Phone: (305) 538-1663
Website: www.holocaustmemorialmiamibeach.org

The saddest or arguably most historically important site in this
book is surely the Holocaust Memorial. Importantly, this a
memorial to the Holocaust, not a museum. As a curator explains,
"Most have no cemetery to visit those family members who
perished in the Holocaust. This is holy ground. It is a place to pay
respects to those who died."[24]
   It began with an idea in 1984 among a small group of Holocaust
survivors to build a memorial. They believed Miami Beach was
an ideal location, as South Florida was home to many survivors.
Given the high number of survivors in the area, the location
seemed right. In the mid-1980s, a *Miami Herald* article estimated
there were twenty thousand to twenty-five thousand survivors in
the region.
   But not all agreed on the need for a memorial. Some felt the
memorial was too somber for the vacation and "fun in the sun"
Miami Beach. "Gloom is doom! Don't turn one of this city's few
bright spots into a cemetery," said Miami Beach Garden Club
member Florence Shubim.[25] Others saw it as a religious symbol on
public land, thereby violating church-state separation laws.
   Advocates for the memorial pleaded their case to the Miami Beach
Planning Board in November 1984. Some made their case in Yiddish

through a translator. The board ended up approving the memorial with a unanimous vote. The city commission followed suit.

The building of the memorial in Miami Beach was to be a reality.

The location of the new memorial had an inner meaning. It had a physical address of 1933-1945 Meridian Avenue—these street numbers corresponded to the years 1933-1945, the period of the Nazi's regime against Jews. Some say this location was fated.

The planners asked architect Kenneth Treister to design the memorial. It was a monumental task. Triester reflected on the enormity of his architectural challenge: "Imagine you're in a concentration camp in Poland surrounded by the Nazis, no communication with the outside world and you're suffering and you're a martyr, you're giving up your life. Each one probably died thinking that no one would ever care, no one would ever know, no one would ever remember."[26]

The memorial's literature describes the draft sketches. "Treister's initial sketches showed an outstretched arm, reaching for the skies as hundreds of small human figures cling to it and to each other. Other early drawings show emaciated people reaching out for help, a naked woman holding onto her baby and a small child, huddled and crying under a blanket."[27]

Above and opposite: Holocaust Memorial in Miami Beach, a sacred ground for many survivors of the Holocaust and their families. (Photos by Aaron Davidson.)

The design was met with resistance. Some felt it was over the top. Others called it a "brutal intrusion on the cityscape." But that was the point. It needed to be something to capture attention.

Treister's design eventually won out. The bronze sculpture was made in Mexico City over a two-year period. In all, the memorial took over four years to complete. By February 1990, it opened to the public. The late Elie Wiesel, a famed writer and Holocaust survivor, spoke at the inauguration.

He said in this speech, "Look at his face. Look at all the faces. Look and you will realize that there existed a suffering that transcended suffering. Woe unto us, for the tragedy which this museum is trying to integrate is beyond words, and beyond imagination, but not beyond memory. And only those who were there know, will know, what it meant being there."[28]

The memorial offers innovative programming. It offers educators a chance to study at Yad Vashem in partnership with the memorial. Another program, Young Lion of Judah, arranges consistent one-on-one meetings of students and survivors and beautification projects at the Holocaust Memorial.

Tips for the Traveler: Take your time at this site. Read the various texts mounted on the wall as you walk through. The descriptions are succinct yet powerful and educational. Observe the statues and what they represent.

You can do a self-guided tour. Ask inside for a brochure. The suggested donation is $2.

While inside, feel free to ask the staff questions. They are friendly and eager to help. You can also purchase DVDs about the Holocaust; sales benefit the memorial.

If your group is ten people or larger, make a reservation online before visiting. I strongly recommend that you inquire about special programming for larger groups. In some cases, the memorial will show a film, offer a tour, and introduce a survivor of the Holocaust. Call the memorial for details and pricing. They also offer a program for educators and their students.

You can also write about your experience on the visitor blog on the memorial's website. It can be an essay, short story, or poem about your experience. This is a great exercise for students who visit the museum.

Even if you don't write anything, I recommend you visit the website and read entries on the blog.

Museums and Performing Arts Centers

Bass Museum of Art
2100 Collins Avenue
Phone: (786) 436-8133
Website: www.thebass.org

Its location is unlikely. In the heart of Miami Beach, one would not expect to find Renaissance and Baroque art. But this is the oldest museum in Miami Beach. It was founded in 1963 by the donations of Jewish art collectors John and Johanna Bass. They bestowed about five hundred works, mostly European old master paintings. In 2002, the museum doubled in size. In 2015, it underwent extensive renovations.

Today, the museum houses European paintings and sculptures from the fifteenth century to the present. Yet its collection is not limited to Europe. It also features Latin American, Asian, and Caribbean art. Less known is its design history of Miami Beach.

The Bass Museum occupies the 1930s Miami Beach Public Library and Art Center designed by Russell Pancoast. He was the grandson of John Collins, one of the key pioneers of the beach.

New World Center
500 17th Street
Phone: (305) 673-3330
Website: www.nws.edu

Designed by Frank Gehry in 2011, the New World Center hosts the famed New World Symphony. But it's more than a concert hall: it is an academy to train top musicians to one day play in orchestras worldwide. The center says it has helped launch the careers of more than 950 alumni worldwide.

Michael Tilson Thomas is its founder and music director. The apple does not fall far from the tree, as the saying goes. He is the grandson of Yiddish theater actors Boris and Bessie Thomashefsky.

Tips for the Traveler: I recommend an in-person, docent-led tour. Call or visit the website ahead of your visit to make a reservation. For just $5, you will learn much more about the institution during the forty-five minute tour. The center also accepts group and private tours.

Another gem is yoga mornings. Try this monthly outdoor class in Vinyassa yoga. Beginners are welcome, and no tickets are needed. Just show up with your mat.

Check the website for concert performances. When attending a conference, consider dining at Thierry's. Located on the first level of the atrium, it is run under the watchful eyes of owner and chef Thierry Isambert. Some of the menu is French cuisine, but Isambert experiments with adding Caribbean or Asian flavors.

Jackie Gleason Theater (The Fillmore Miami Beach at the Jackie Gleason Theater)
1700 Washington Avenue
Phone: (305) 673-7300
Website: www.fillimoremb.com

"To the moon, Alice!"

It began in 1950 as the Fillmore Miami Beach Municipal Auditorium. Entertainment varied from singing to comedy sketches to boxing. Celebrities often came to watch performances.

In the 1960s, variety shows on television began to take off. The auditorium successfully hosted the Dick Clark Show and Miss Universe Pageants.

Then, in 1964, city planners had an idea. Why not ask the star Jackie Gleason to film his show from this location? This would transform the venue into an iconic production center for a show that millions of viewers would tune into weekly. The top-rated *Jackie Gleason Show* was broadcast from the venue for many years. In some ways, it put Miami Beach, as an entertainment center, on the map. Gleason always promoted Miami Beach on camera as being the "fun and sun capital of the world" and proclaimed Miami Beach audiences as the "greatest in the world."

A typical episode would open with a splashy dance number

followed by an opening monologue. Gleason would then saunter towards the edge of the stage and clap his hands, singing, "And away we go!" Comedy sketches followed. Some were recurring characters often based on Gleason's real life experiences. One such character was the cantankerous bus driver Ralph Kramden, who was the subject of *The Honeymooners.*

In the 1970s, the venue was renovated extensively and was renamed Miami Beach Theater of the Performing Arts. Broadway tours performed there as they traveled throughout Florida.

Trends in names of venues change. In 1987, Jackie Gleason died. The city decided to rename the theater the Jackie Gleason Theater of the Performing Arts.

Notable Eateries

Havana 1957 Cuban Cuisine
405 Espanola Way
Phone: (305) 503-3828
Website: www.havana1957.com

Take a trip back to 1950s Cuba at this establishment. There are a few locations, the one on Espanola Way being one of the most famous. Everything here is classic Cuban: the food, music, and vintage memorabilia. Look around the restaurant, including the ceiling and the floor, and you'll see prints of legendary figures of mid-twentieth-century Cuba. Try a mojito and one of the house specialties. The restaurant is known for its Pollo Havana 1957 (traditional roasted chicken in a sumptuous Cuban gravy). For desert, try the guava cheesecake. The website displays a stylish video of the food against a backdrop of Cuban jazz music. Take a look.

Yardbird Southern Table and Bar
1600 Lenox Avenue
Phone: (305) 538-5220
Website: www.runchickenrun.com

Though Miami Beach may not seem like the South, it is. So you should try some Southern cooking at Yardbird. Enjoy smoked barbeque chicken, fried green tomatoes, grits, and deviled eggs. The restaurant is known for its Mama's Biscuits, on which you can have honey butter or house-made jam. Of course, the fried chicken is classic. If you prefer fish, Yardbird offers smoked trout with dill and chives. If you like the venue and find yourself in Las Vegas, there is a branch there too.

Middle Beach (40th-75th Street Neighborhood)

The area around 41st street is the heart of contemporary Jewish life in Miami Beach. It is worth a visit to see some of the shops, eateries, markets, and schools. On Friday afternoon, you will see religious families preparing for the Sabbath.

Educational Institutions

Hebrew Day Academy
2400 Pine Tree Drive
Phone: (305) 532-6421
Website: www.rasg.org

Rabbi Alexander S. Gross founded the Hebrew Academy in 1947 as the first Orthodox Jewish day school south of Baltimore. In that year, it was located at 1 Lincoln Road in two rooms in a YMHA. Soon after, more space was needed for the growing student body. The Hebrew Academy then bought a building that had been a Methodist Church at 6th Street and Jefferson Avenue for $45,000. The curriculum was bilingual in English and Hebrew.

Today, it serves approximately six hundred students from preschool through twelfth grade and is considered modern Orthodox. Its vision is to "inspire and equip students to achieve their greatest potential academically and spiritually by focusing on their individual attributes and instilling eternal Torah values in a changing world."[29]

Talmudic University
4000 Alton Road
Phone: (305) 534-7050
Website: www.talmudicu.edu

Opened in 1974, the Talmudic University is an Orthodox yeshiva.

Located on the site of an old Howard Johnson hotel at 41st and Alton Road, it provides classes, lectures, and study groups to the public and to those of various Jewish affiliations.

Stores

Kastner's Market
700 Arthur Godfrey Road
Phone: (305) 535-2255
Website: www.kastnersmarket.com

Stroll down the aisles of this kosher supermarket listening to the Hebrew music playing. It offers items not commonly found in other supermarkets, like roll mops herring (the kind that wraps around a toothpick), Hungarian cabbage, unsalted borscht, and much more.

In 2007, Aaron and Rachel Wasser bought the existing business and expanded it.

Torah Treasures
534 Arthur Godfrey Road
Phone: (305) 673-6095
Website: www.torahtreasuresmiami.com

This store's tagline is the Department Store for Judaica. It sells mostly books on religious topics, as well as prayer and ritual merchandise like Seder plates.

Notable Eateries

Roasters and Toasters
525 41st Street
Phone: (305) 531-7691
http://roastersntoasters.com

This upbeat kosher-style deli features all the classic styles you would expect. It has two other locations in Aventura and Miami.

Its name derives from its origins as a coffee shop that roasted its own beans. Al and Sandy Burger were the owners in 1984. The couple came up with an idea that they would eventually have patented: a bagel ball. Bagel balls are rounded bagels sometimes stuffed with cream cheese.

By the mid-1990s, the enterprising couple sold the coffee shop to Jack Kantrowitz and Dan Kaplan. They saw an opportunity to turn the fledgling coffee house into a deli.

While it is proving a success, tragedy intervened. Jack Kantrowitz died in a tragic motorcycle accident. Five years later, the restaurant suffered a major fire. But it reopened, and business recovered.

Tips for the Traveler: Take a look at the iconic pictures on the wall. You will see classic film stars and scenes like Audrey Hepburn in *Breakfast at Tiffany's*.

I recommend the smoked fish platter. You can choose up to three items. Select from Nova, Belly Lox, Sable, Whitefish, Herring in Wine or Cream Sauce, Herring Salad, Whitefish Salad, or Salmon Salad. Plus, it comes with a bagel, cream cheese, lettuce, tomato, and onions.

Roasters and Toasters is open for breakfast and lunch. Like most delis in the area, it closes around 3:30 p.m.

Miami Chocolates
456 41st Street
Phone: (305) 222-7003
Website: www.miamibeachchocolates.com

Opened by a mother and son team in 2009, Miami Chocolates is a must-visit for the chocolate lover—and that basically includes everyone.

The store offers four kinds of chocolates: vegan, dairy-free, sugar free, and chocolate-covered fruits. Like many chocolate shops, it offers gift baskets and catering. The chocolates are kosher.

I recommend you take the tours of the factory. You'll learn the history of this wonderful treat and how it is produced. Ask about learning the techniques for dipping pretzels and marshmallows into chocolate. The tour is hands on . . . literally.

They also offer a program called Sweet Night Out. You will learn to decorate your own treats and build chocolate masterpieces. It can make a fun gift, family outing, or corporate event.

Historic Synagogues

Temple Beth Israel
770 W. 40th Street
Phone: (305) 538-1251
Website: bethisraelmiami.org

Founded in 1954 in a storefront, the congregation began to service snowbirds, or winter-only residents. After being housed in three different storefronts, the founders bought the current site and dramatically renovated the original building. For decades, this was the only Orthodox congregation in the Miami Beach area. It is still one of the largest.

In 2012, a major change took place when Temple Beth Israel merged with the Young Israel of Miami Beach.

Temple Beth Shalom
4144 Chase Avenue
Phone: (305) 538-7231
Website: www.tbsmb.org

This is the largest and oldest Reform synagogue in Miami Beach. It started with reading a Yiddish newspaper.

Abraham Zinnamon saw Benjamin Appel reading a Yiddish newspaper. One thing led to another and the two were engaged in a conversation on creating a Reform congregation. The year was 1942.

The first services were held in a storefront, which was not unusual for a new congregation. They built their congregation step-by-step—literally. The rabbi Leon Kronish knocked on doors in neighborhoods and invited Jewish families to join the new synagogue. The budding congregation changed locations several times and by the 1960s had grown to more than twelve hundred families. The rabbi emphasized its communal role in addition to its religious one. During the tumultuous 1960s civil rights protests, the congregation was involved. Kronish served as rabbi until 1984. He was succeeded by Rabbi Gary Glickstein, who still serves.

Community Centers

Jewish Community Center
4221 Pine Tree Drive
Phone: (305) 534-3206
Website: www.mbjcc.org

This JCC offers cultural programming, fitness activities, community services, and programs specifically for children, adults, and seniors.

Notable Hotels

Two iconic hotels designed by Morris Lapidus have been at the center of Miami Beach nightlife and glamour since the 1950s.

Eden Roc Hotel
4525 Collins Avenue
Phone: (305) 531-0000
Website: www.nobuedenroc.com

Next door to the Fontainebleau is the Eden Roc, designed by Morris Lapidus. Completed in 1956, the hotel is in the Miami modern style, which was popular at the time. Located on Millionaire's Row, the site was home to the Warner Brother's Albert Warner of film fame.

Lapidus designed the hotel for a tough Harry Mufson. Less than impressed with the Fontainebleau, Mufson made his wishes clear. "I don't want any of the French stuff you used at the Fontainebleau. That's for kids." Paradoxically, the hotel was named for the Eden Roc pavilion at the Hotel du Cap-Eden-Roc in Antibes, France.

There was no love lost between hotelier Ben Novack of the Fontainebleau and Mufson. In fact, their relationship soured badly. Novack felt wronged by Mufson and built a blank seventeen-story wing as a "spite wall" on the Fontainebleau property to shade the Eden Roc's pool. This inspired a drawn-out court battle. Eventually, the courts sided with the Fontainebleau. Eden Roc responded by building new pools in locations that could still get sunshine.

Mufson purposely avoided the "sweeping curves" of the Fontainebleau. He preferred a "more formal composition" prominent among area hotels of earlier decades.[30]

Less flashy than its neighbor, the lesser-known Eden Roc boasted the Café Pompei, a supper club where diners would also view entertainment. Mufson established his legacy with the eponymous Harry's American Bar, which served as the hotel's nightclub.

Marriott International took over operations in 2005 under the Renaissance Hotels and Resorts Brand. It did not go well. The relationship between the owners and Marriott was less than friendly. Lawsuits ensued. By 2013, Marriott pulled out. Eden Roc then became part of Destination Hotels and Resorts.

Can you guess what landmark hit TV comedy series featured the hotel in several episodes? The hint is that it is considered the second sitcom on TV.

The hotel is in *I Love Lucy*. Lucy and Ricky Ricardo and their neighbors, the Mertzes, stay in this hotel.

Tips for the Traveler: The hotel is pet-friendly. Bring your furry friend!

Search the property's website and third party sites for specials and package deals. They are not as rare as one may think.

Hike the nearby five-mile nature preserve. The hotel offers water sports like jet skiing, surfing, waterskiing, and kayaking.

Fontainebleau Hotel
4441 Collins Avenue
Phone: (305) 535-3283
Website: www.fontainebleau.com

Nestled in the heart of Millionaire's Row, Fontainebleau Miami Beach harkens back to the era of glamorous hotels and luxury. Noted hotelier Ben Novack purchased the Firestone Mansion, home of the king of auto tires, Harvey Firestone, in 1952 for $2.3 million. Designed by Morris Lapidus in 1954, it is one of the area's most famous hotels. It is best known for its stylish dining choices, nightlife, and spa treatments.

Lapidus once wrote a wise statement that encapsulated human nature and its quest for glamor. He foresaw the need for a place like Fontainebleau, writing, "If you create a stage and it is grand, everyone who enters will play their part."

For decades, the hotel was recognizable enough that a sign was unneeded. But that did not last. In 1977, the hotel declared bankruptcy. One year later, it was rescued; Stephen Muss purchased it for $27 million (about $100 million in today's dollars). He renovated it extensively for about $100 million and hired Hilton to manage it.

In 2005, Muss sold the Fontainebleau to Turnberry Associates for $165 million. Given that amount and the cost of repairs, it does not seem like an impressive return on investment. It seemed that Lapidus was right in that a luxurious setting would attract visitors, but that did not mean the business would be profitable.

The hotel is noted for something completely unrelated to hoteling. Trial lawyers for real estate claims know it for the landmark 1959 case *Fontainebleau Hotel Corp vs. Forty-Five Twenty-Five, Inc.* The case was decided by the Florida District Courts of Appeal. Essentially, Eden Roc Hotel next door sued Fontainebleau for a proposed expansion that would block sunlight into Eden Roc Hotel's swimming pool.

Several years and many dollars later, the courts ruled in Fontainebleau's favor.

Much of the hotel was closed in 2006 for a few years as it was expanded and new condominiums were built. It reopened in late 2008. Unfortunately, that was during the heart of the financial crisis.

The hotel has been portrayed in many films, like those with Frank Sinatra and Elvis Presley. It was also in James Bond's *Goldfinger*. The 1971 hit comedy *Bananas* from Woody Allen features a reference when the fleeing dictator of a made-up country calls the Fontainebleau for a room reservation.

Its more recent pop-culture cameos include references in *The Sopranos, Top Chef,* and the Victoria's Secret Fashion Show.

Tips for the Traveler: I recommend sitting in the lounge and ordering drinks. Admire the beautiful motifs and style. It features "a 17,000-square-foot lobby with the now-legendary *Stairway to Nowhere*, six acres of formal gardens designed to replicate Versailles and thousands of dollars in antique furnishings to authentically convey the hotel's French period theme."[31]

Try one of the restaurants: Stripsteak for excellent meat, Scarpetta for Italian, or Hakkasan for Cantonese. Blade Sushi also gets rave reviews.

Many visit and stay in the hotel for the lively nightlife. This ranges from bars to lounges to dance clubs. LIV and Bleaulive are well known. Be aware that they have a dress code.

Check the website for cyber specials. Sometimes, there are discounts for up to 25% off rooms with restrictions in dates. Look for spa discounts, too. Note that there is daily charge on top of the official hotel room and tax. Don't be surprised when you get your bill.

The add-ons at Fontainebleau are very expensive. This includes in-room services and amenities as well as food, snacks, or services you may purchase around the property. Ask about the price before you commit to avoid sticker shock.

There is a beach area, which I recommend. You can rent umbrellas and chairs, but it probably only pays to do that if you start early. If you come to the beach at 4 p.m., for example, you still have to pay for the entire day, and the service ends around 5 p.m.

North Beach (75th Street Northward)

Sites of Famous Places Now Gone

Site of Pumpernik's

Pumpernik's is another Jewish deli opened by Wilfred Cohen (a.k.a. "Wolfie," who also started the deli Wolfie's). Located at Collins Avenue and 67th Street, the classic Jewish deli enjoyed its heyday in the 1950s and 1960s. It opened in other locations, including North Miami, Hallandale, and Fort Lauderdale.

Radio star Larry King broadcast his first local talk radio show each morning from this Miami Beach location.

Charles Linksman and his family eventually owned and ran the delis. Linksman died in 1990. His son, Mark, gave up the deli business to become a yoga instructor in San Diego, California. His career choice mirrors a larger trend: in the past decades, consumers have eschewed delis for what they consider healthier food. Whether people are, in fact, living more healthfully is up for debate.

Pumpernik's closed in the 1990s but still had remaining locations in the area. However, those too eventually went out of business.

Site of Wolfie Cohen's Rascal House

Another classic Jewish deli, Rascal House was located at Collins Avenue and 172nd Street in Sunny Isles. It opened in 1954 and closed in 2008. The restaurant featured a sign that said, "The only thing that needs to come dressed is our chickens!" Patrons were still required to wear clothes; the saying meant that dress was casual.

Patrons remember the large neon sign in the front—back in the deli's founding decade, the Miami modern style was popular. The food extended beyond the restaurant walls. Pan American Airlines served Wolfie's famous cheesecake on flights to New York, and patrons of Northeast Airlines were served Wolfie's food exclusively.

Some core customers were early eaters and liked saving a few bucks. To accommodate this market, Rascal House offered an early bird menu from 3 p.m. to 6 p.m.

The founder, Wolfie Cohen, also started the equally famous Pumpernik's and Wolfie's.

Rascal House thrived in the 1950s and 1960s with a more elderly Jewish population, a common market for delis. Yet in the 1970s and 1980s and beyond, this trend reversed. Many moved to counties to the north and others passed away. Business suffered. Changing consumer tastes also hastened the decline. Diners were

An ad for *Wolfie Cohen's Rascal House Restaurant* on *Miami Beach Motel Row.* (From the collections of the Jewish Museum of Florida-FIU, originated by Marcia Jo Zerivitz, founding executive director.)

looking for smaller portions and something they perceived as healthier.

The weather did not help. In 2005, Hurricane Wilma hurt the famed Rascal House sign and building. The sign was replaced, but it lacked the visual appeal of its predecessor.

Sadly, Rascal House closed in 2008. The site was converted to Epicure Market and a condo building. However, developers looking to make a quick buck were caught in the financial crisis of 2009, and the condo project was put on hold.

What 1980s hit sitcom set in Miami featured references to Wolfie's and to Rascal House? The answer is *Golden Girls.* Characters referred to dining there.

The final night of Rascal House in late 2008 was grim. Oldtimers felt they were losing something special. Some patrons called it "the last supper." Memorabilia was auctioned the next day. Newspaper reports described it: "The red counter stools were empty. Wide plastic menus sold for $25 each. Platters once full of food cost $5. Patrons stopped by to stare in the windows through cupped hand or to buy some small piece of the restaurant they loved."[32]

Items auctioned included a photo of Jackie Gleason and a sign with the Rascal House logo.

Historic Synagogues

Temple Menorah
620 75th Street
Phone: (305) 866-2156
Website: www.tmjm.org

Called the North Shore Jewish Center, it began in a storefront in nearby Normandy Isles in 1949. Rabbi Mayer Abramowitz led the small community. In the 1950s, it secured its current location, and by decade's end, it was renamed Temple Menorah to encapsulate "Jewish leadership, education and community on the Beach."[33]

During this time, Temple Menorah partnered with the Hebrew Immigrant Aid Society in aiding Holocaust survivors. South Florida received a large percentage of survivors. By the 1960s, the congregation was trying to settle "Jubans," or Cuban Jews fleeing from Castro's Cuba. To this day, Temple Menorah is known for having taken an active role in helping settle the Cuban Jews while many other congregations were perceived as indifferent to their plight.

In 1962, the building underwent renovation by none other than Morris Lapidus. By this time, he was well-known as an architect through designs of places like Fontainebleau.

Temple Menorah has also been involved with interfaith outreach. The Lutheran Church uses the facilities as well.

The year 1972 was unique for Miami Beach. Both the Democrat and Republican conventions were held there. Given the tumultuous 1968 conventions, many were worried about safety. The temple stepped in to "act as an intermediary between law enforcement."[34] It also housed student activists in its banquet facilities.

The current rabbi has an interesting slogan for a service he provides. The program is called the Rabbi's Challenge, and its slogan is Have Knowledge, Will Travel. A congregant chooses a topic, and the rabbi will visit their home or other place for an informal class.

Temple Menorah, which began as a storefront in 1949 and played a key role in settling Cuban Jews fleeing from Castro's Cuba. (Photo by Aaron Davidson.)

Temple Moses
1200 Normandy Drive
Phone: (305) 868-6124
Website: www.templemoses.com

This striking synagogue emerged from the Sephardic tradition. The congregation began in the 1960s by Cuban Jewish refugees from Cuba. The Orthodox congregation sought to "create Temple Moses as a living monument to its plight."[35] A plaque by the front entrance notes, "We will never forget what we left behind on the island of Cuba." Many congregants' ancestry is from Turkey and Cuba. Today, the community follows the rituals and traditions from congregations once in these two countries. Part of its mission is to preserve and celebrate this heritage.

The rabbi explains that the congregation is "not so much a Cuban synagogue as a Turkish one." He notes, "This is the genuine community of Judeo-Spanish Jews. Their culture is connected to that of Spain. Other Sephardic Jews may have ancestry from Spain, yet their culture is more Middle Eastern. In contrast, this

Temple Moses bimah, a congregation of Judeo-Spanish Jews. (Photo by Aaron Davidson.)

congregation has maintained the food, culture, heritage, songs, and other traditions of the Spanish European heritage."[36]

Services are conducted in English and Hebrew, but some parts, including some songs and prayers, are also in Ladino. Derived from Old Spanish, Ladino was spoken in the Ottoman Empire territories. That included Turkey, Greece, and countries in the Middle East and regions within North Africa. Most Jews arrived in these parts in 1492 when they were exiled from Spain in the Spanish Inquisition. Though less known in the United States than Yiddish, Ladino is spoken among certain groups in Balkan countries, Israel, Turkey, and France. Sadly, the language is threatened with extinction as most speakers are elderly and their progeny have generally not learned it. But, like Yiddish, it is experiencing a minor revival, particularly in music and in folktales.

Another example of continuing these traditions is in food. At social events, food served includes bulemas (spinach roles in phyllo), biscochos (cookies with cinnamon and ginger), and filo (wheat flower dough).

Tips for the Traveler: If possible, attend a service. The sanctuary has a beautifully made bimah with Torah scrolls displayed, lions on either side of the ark, and silk coverings for the Torah scrolls. The twelve tribes of Israel are displayed in the stained glass.

Notable Eateries and Shops

Goldstein's Prime
7419 Collins Avenue
Phone: (305) 865-2992
Website: www.goldsteinsprime.com

It's the last of its kind in the North Beach neighborhood. In the 1980s, Goldstein and Sons Kosher Meats drew lots of customers. Other kosher butcher shops abounded. Customers would come from afar to stock up on kosher meats, fish, poultry, and side items.

In recent years, Goldstein's business has been challenged. Though competition is light, chains like Costco and online retailers

The last of its kind in the North Beach neighborhood, Goldstein's Prime endures in a changing neighborhood and competitive industry. (Photo by Aaron Davidson.)

have drawn away customers. Supermarkets also now offer kosher meats. Convenience- and price-oriented shoppers are choosing alternatives. The demographics of the neighborhood have changed unfavorably for the business as well.

Still, Goldstein's Prime endures, at least for now. A sign on a shelf reads Our Finest Cuts.

Shop for take-out items like to-go soups (mushroom barley, vegetable, split pea, chicken broth), kugels (noodle, potato, spinach) and kasha varnishkas. In addition to meats, poultry, and turkey, Goldstein's Prime also offers fish. Selections include sea bass, tuna, wild salmon, homemade gravlax, and snapper.

I recommend the homemade sandwiches. They are made to order, and there is seating in the front. Try the Israeli turkey sandwich.

David's Bakery
7423 Collins Avenue
Phone: (305) 867-2317
Website: www.davidskosherbakerymiamibeach.com

Next door to Goldstein's Prime is David's Bakery, which replaced a previous bakery on this site. It's still an old-fashioned bakery. No skinny lattes or gluten-free desserts are served here. I'm not sure that the staff would even know what those are. The small bakery seems to harken to a simpler time.

I recommend the apple strudel. Also try the breads and various flavored challahs. If you would like something sweet after your sandwich at Goldstein's Prime next door, go for the traditional cakes. Choose between marble, sponge, cheese, or raspberry elegant. Apparently, the most popular is Boston cake.

David's Bakery, an old-fashioned bakery known for its flavored challahs and apple strudel. (Photo by Aaron Davidson.)

Notable Hotels

Deauville Hotel
6701 Collins Avenue
Phone: (800) 327-6656
Website: www.deauvillebeachresortmiami.com

Architect Melvin Grossman designed this 1957 hotel. It was a time of glamor and style for hotels, showcased in the Fontainebleau and Eden Roc. Deauville was considered a "favorite of celebrities including Frank Sinatra, Dean Martin and Sammy Davis Jr."[37]

In 1964, it made international headlines. The highly viewed *Ed Sullivan Show* featured a performance here by the Beatles. Clips from that performance are shown even today.

In the mid-1980s, the sixteen-story hotel converted rooms into individual condo units. It became a condo-hotel.

Since then, as a beach resort, it has never recaptured its former glory. It has also run into significant violations related to the "physical condition of the structural systems and life-safety issues of the resort."[38]

Chapter Three

Miami

Though Miami has a sizeable Jewish population today, it was among the last communities in Florida to establish a sizeable Jewish population. It may come as a surprise to learn that the City of Miami was not incorporated until 1896. At that time, Jews owned twelve of the original sixteen businesses. A population of 30,000 (that included 100 Jewish families) exploded to more than 130,000 with 3,500 Jews by 1925. Jews founded temples and cemeteries and were among those who chartered the University of Miami in 1925. More Jews emigrated to the new city, and real estate prices shot up—only to be interrupted by the devastating hurricane of 1926. Yet Miami's recovery was swift. By the 1930s through the 1950s, Shenandoah became a vibrant Jewish neighborhood. By the 1960s, many Jews moved to northern suburbs and to Broward and Palm Beach Counties. The area around Shenandoah became Little Havana. The Jewish population became an interesting mix of Cuban Jews (both Askenazi and Sephardim), snowbirds, Jews from other Latin American countries, and those with ancestral roots in the Iberian Peninsula where Ladino was spoken.

But by the 1980s, as Miami became known to some as the new "Ellis Island for people fleeing troubled countries," the Jewish population declined.[1] This outflow, though, was counterbalanced by Jews from Latin America, Russia, and Israel. Within Miami, many Jews moved out of downtown. This trend continued into the 2000s. Downtown became undesirable.

After a steady decline in the Jewish population from the mid-1970s to the mid-2000s, Miami-Dade's Jewish population increased by about 9 percent from 2004 to 2014. A new young-adult Jewish population of about 7,000 sprang up in Miami's downtown. The largest increase, 17 percent, was in those under 35. Hispanic Jews in Miami grew by 57 percent during this period, with most from Argentina, Venezuela, Columbia, and Peru. Perhaps the largest driver was the increase in Orthodox Jewish households at 41 percent.[2]

The last decade has seen an increase in the Jewish cultural revival of Miami's downtown. On your travels, you will see new museums and restaurants, energized congregations, and vibrant ethnic neighborhoods.

Visit the historic Temple Beth David and Temple Israel and marvel at the architecture. Be sure to visit the City of Miami Cemetery's Jewish section to see the burial places of some of the city's earliest Jewish pioneers. Walk the ethnic neighborhoods of the once-Jewish area of Little Havana, where you can sample Cuban food and coffee and hear Latin jazz. See some of city's oldest sites at Coconut Grove. Take in the unique art at the Perez Art Museum and the sprawling estates of Vizcaya and Deering Estate at Cutler.

Museums

These museums are Jewish-related either by their founders, focus, or occasional exhibits.

Patricia and Phillip Frost Museum of Science
1101 Biscayne Boulevard
Phone: (305) 434-9600
Website: www.frostscience.org

The Frost Museum of Science opened in 2016. It seeks to "inspire people of all ages and cultures to enjoy science and technology, in order to better understand ourselves and our world."[3]

The museum began in 1949 with an imperative: Dade County's children need a science museum. After switching locations, by 1952 it had become the Museum of Science and Natural History.

It expanded and provided more exhibits in subsequent decades. In 2016, it opened its new home next to the recently built Perez Art Museum.

The philanthropist Philip Frost grew up in an observant Jewish family. Much of his career was in public health, serving at the National Cancer Institute in the mid-1960s and as an academic at the University of Miami School of Dermatology.

Frost endowed the School of Music at the University of Miami, the Art Museum at Florida International University, and, more recently, the Miami Science Museum, which was renamed the Patricia and Phillip Frost Science Museum. Frost's endowment also benefitted the associated planetarium. (See chapter 6 for more on Phillip Frost.)

Perez Art Museum
1103 Biscayne Boulevard
Phone: (305) 375-3000
Website: www.pamm.org
Hours: Mon.–Tues., 10a.m.–6 p.m.; Thurs., 10 a.m.–9 p.m.; Fri.-Sun., 10 a.m.–6 p.m.
Admission: Adults $16

As you drive along the Biscayne Bay, you will come across an eye-catching three-story structure made to look like Stillsville, a group of wooden houses built on stilts. A vertical garden of local plants outlines the exterior. The vast building, the Perez Art Museum, is part of the new Museum Park downtown that will also house the new Miami Science Museum.

Swiss architects Herzog and de Meuron designed the recently built museum. Its beauty is derived from its nature-inspired façade.

The museum, which recently opened on this site, showcases contemporary art. It was built in 2011 for $220 million. Originally the Center for Fine Arts, it changed its name to the simpler Miami Art Museum. In 2013, it was renamed for Latin American art collector Jorge Perez.

Its permanent collections showcase work from well-known contemporary artists like Frank Stella and Kiki Smith. (Smith was instrumental in the restoration of the famed Eldridge Street Museum in New York through her work on the window in the sanctuary.) Cuban painters like Jose Valdes and Mexican artists like Diego Rivera also have a strong presence in the museum thanks to Perez's donations.

The museum is trying to showcase artists from diverse backgrounds. Perez pledged money for a fund to acquire noteworthy African American art.

The museum was not established without drama. One episode sounds like a scene from a bad reality show rather than from a high-brow museum opening. A vociferous critic attacked the museum for not showing enough local artists. Maximo Caminero smashed a Chinese vase in protest. The vase was estimated at $1 million. Caminero was charged with criminal conduct and pled guilty to one charge of criminal misconduct. Yet his sentence was light. He was placed on probation for eighteen months and was given one hundred hours of community service—not bad for smashing a million bucks. The museum noted that his presence is unwelcome at the museum during his probation.

Part of the museum's charm is its interaction with the natural. Hanging gardens adorn the outside. The views provide picturesque views of the Biscayne Bay. The huge second-floor windows allow for natural sunlight and stunning views. It's as though nature is interacting with the art for the viewer's experience.

Museum literature explains the interweaving of outdoor space, nature, and the viewer experience. "The canopy's overhang creates a series of outdoor spaces that bridge the museum, park and city. The canopy is perforated to allow in light and lush vegetation amongst the columns transforms the veranda into a multi-dimensional garden. The tropical plants enfolding the museum are integral to the experience. The design allows for multiple transitions, as visitors gradually move from the outside to the inside, hot to cold, humid to dry, and from the street or park to the art."[4]

The first floor concentrates on rotating installation exhibits. Tour guides point out compelling questions. For example, some photographs capture everyday life. Several of these photos have fetched a lot of money in auctions. Yet, subjects were never paid, while artists and galleries made a handsome profit. Though legal, the exhibit asks if this is ethical.

The museum has also shown some Jewish artists. An example is Yael Bartana, an Israeli-born artist exploring social themes through art. Her work *Inferno* debuted at this museum. It considered the "rise of Evangelism in Brazil and its connections to the 'Holy Land' and Judaic traditions and history."[5] Her work references a construction of the third Temple of Solomon in Sao Paulo by a Neo-Pentecostal Church in the late-1970s.

You can inquire about plans for any future exhibits.

Tips for the Traveler: I highly recommend at least one tour. They are offered three times per day and are included in admission. Some tours may be less frequent, so call ahead to inquire. There are three types of tours:

Architecture: This tour is worth it to learn more about the award-winning interior and exterior space. Construction buffs can ask about materials used. It also covers gardens and their use on the exterior building.

Global Positioning Systems: I recommend this tour for understanding the cultural and political context of works. For example, on my tour, the guide asked, "What are the ethics of a photographer taking pictures of people without their knowledge?" In viewing artwork of Australian aborigines, the tour explored elders, tribes, and communications of the divine through art.

Museum Highlights: This is the "survey course" of the collections and architecture. If your group is small, the subjects can be somewhat customized to your interests.

Private tours are also available, as are tours in Spanish. Inquire at the front desk. Note that the museum is open until 9 p.m. on Thursdays.

For lunch or dinner, consider the Verde restaurant on the ground floor of the museum. You can elect either to take out and eat outside, gazing at the tranquil views of the Biscayne Bay, or dine at the restaurant itself.

It's not a typical rush-and-go museum restaurant. The menu is extensive and offers specialty cocktails and wines.

Rubell Family Collection
95 NW 29th Street
Phone: (305) 573-6090
Website: rfc.museum
Hours: Vary; check the website for updated information

From its humble beginnings in 1964 when founders Donald and Mera Rubell slowly bought contemporary art with their weekly savings, the Rubell Family Collection is today one of the world's largest privately owned contemporary art collections.

In 1993, the collection relocated to Miami. It's housed in a prodigious 45,000 square-foot building that once belonged to the Drug Enforcement Agency, who stored confiscated goods in the once crime-ridden Wynwood Arts District of Miami. In 1994, the family expanded the collection's mission to include a public contemporary art museum. Artists showcased read like a Who's Who in contemporary art: Keith Haring, Jean-Michel Basquiat, and Jeff Koons, among others. The collection works closely with Miami-Dade Public Schools to expand viewership among the young.

There are occasional exhibits with Jewish themes. One example is the four-color Barbra from the Jewish Jackie Series that was acquired in 1992. It features acrylic and screen print on canvas.

The Rubells have been called the art world's game changers, as their impact on culture has been profound. In the early years, the Rubells focused on artists who had not yet been discovered, like Keith Haring. They had an instinct for finding talent. Mera Rubell placed emphasis on visiting-artist studios. She would say, "Art doesn't come to you, you have to go the art."

South Florida Folk Life Center
101 Flagler Street
Phone: (305) 375-1492
Website: www.historymiami.org

This innovative and little-know museum is definitely worth a visit. It explores the cultures of many people and seeks to find commonality among them. One exhibit asks, "What do quinceañera celebrations, Trinidadian steelpan music and breakdancing have in common? What about cigar rolling, Brazilian samba and bluegrass jam sessions? Answer: these cultural traditions are examples of the region's folk life."

Founded in 1986, the center is a division of HistoryMiami. It focuses on "documenting, presenting and supporting local traditional arts and culture."

I recommend the exhibit *Beyond the Game: Sports and Evolution of South Florida*, which looks at how sports spurred tourist and resident growth in the area.

The center also explores Jewish culture. For example, artist

Nancy Billings created textile art for visitors and explored the making of the Jewish wedding canopy, the chuppah. She explained the significance behind the Jewish textiles.

Jewish Cultural Events

Miami Jewish Film Festival
4200 Biscayne Boulevard
Phone: (305) 576-4030
Website: www.caje-miami.org

Held in January, this festival seeks to screen the best of international Jewish cinema for thirteen days at ten venues across Greater Miami. In total, there are about eighty film premiers. Some are from new filmmakers. Check out both feature-length films and shorts at the festival. Movie topics range from portrayals of the famed author Amoz Oz, a Persian-language family drama, the kidnapping of three Jewish teens, and the tale of a washed-up lounge singer.

Alper Jewish Community Center
11155 SW 112th Avenue
Phone: (305) 271-9000
Website: www.alperjcc.org

This innovative Jewish community center offers the Lisa Ann Watson Children's Discovery Museum. Exhibits take complex social topics and make them understandable and relatable for children. For example, the art exhibit *From Home to Home: Jewish Immigration to America* looks at families who made the decision to leave their countries. It portrays their hopes and fears. The hands-on, multi-sensory exhibit makes these journeys come alive for children ages six to twelve. Interactivity is emphasized, including creating art, peeking into dioramas of life in multiple periods and locations, and dressing immigrant children in American clothes.

Also check out the literary and performing arts programs in the Robert Russell Theater. A roster of comedians, musicians, actors, and dancers perform.

Historic Synagogues

Temple Beth David
4657 Hood Road
Phone: (561) 694-2350
Website: www.templebethdavidfl.org

It's the oldest congregation in Miami.

The earliest Jews in Miami came with Henry Flagerler's railroad extension from Palm Beach to Miami in 1896. They worshipped at members' homes with a rabbi from West Palm Beach. Later that year, a fire ravaged through Miami. By 1900, only three Jews remained: Mr. Isidor Cohen and Mr. and Mrs. Joseph Schneidman. Joseph died with a few years. By 1911, five documented Jewish families lived in Miami. They were the families of Isidor Cohen, Harris Schneidman, David Afremows, Morris Zions, and Phillip Ullendorfs. More arrived in subsequent years.

Founded in the early days of Miami, this pioneer synagogue formed from a small congregation. They met in the home of early member Morris Pilkansky and later in the home of Medel Rippa. It was originally named B'nai Zion after Morris Zion, a member who made the largest contribution and became its first president.

Temple Beth David, housing Miami's oldest congregation. (Courtesy Beth David Congregation.)

After witnessing the death of a Jewish visitor, members realized the need for a burial ground. By 1913, it formed a Jewish burial section within the City of Miami Cemetery. The cemetery was located near Shenadoah, a Jewish neighborhood that thrived until the 1960s.

Viewers can visit the Jewish section, which is walled in. A visual distinction is the Hebrew lettering on headstones. The first burial in this section was for early congregant Harry Sachs in 1915. Burials occurred in the section through the 1940s, with the last Jewish burial in 1964. As the Jewish community moved north in later decades, so did their places of burial. Cemeteries used included Mt. Nebo Kendall Memorial Gardens and Mt. Sinai Memorial Park Cemetery.

With the expansion of Henry Flagler's railroad in the region, the once remote area began to grow rapidly. Business opportunities abounded. Under this backdrop, the Jewish population of Miami increased—and so did its need for a formal place of worship and lifecycle rituals. In 1917, the congregation changed its name from B'nai Zion to Beth David, a nod to David Afremow for his financial contribution. Afremow was owner of the famed Miami-based New York Department Store. The store was later sold and re-emerged as Cromer-Cassel's, which later became Richard's Department Store. A board was formed that included one of Miami's first Jewish settlers, Isidor Cohen.

Yet the congregation was itinerant. Housed in various public halls, including the Masonic Temple, they were constantly on the move.

By 1920, the budding congregation had a home. It was in downtown Miami. About two hundred Jewish families lived in the region, but dissension was afoot. Members had varying viewpoints on following rituals and Jewish laws. Some wanted to follow Reform, others Conservative, and still others Orthodox. The schism was growing deeper. At a key meeting in 1921 in the home of Morris Cowen, it was discussed that the temple would use more Reform practices. Rabbi Salo Stein tried to avert conflict by introducing a modern Conservative approach. It did not work. Finally, in 1922, the temple divided. Part of the congregation spun off to form Miami's first Reform congregation: Temple Israel. The remaining part joined the Conservative movement.

In 1925, another group divided and formed the Miami Orthodox Congregation, later renamed Congregation Beth El.

As the population boomed, Beth David thrived. Jewish aid organizations sprung up. These included Hadassah, the National Council of Jewish Women, B'nai B'rith lodge, and the United Jewish Aid Association. The Great Miami Hurricane ravaged the congregation on September 11, 1926, which happened to be Kol Nidre, the night prior to the high holiday of Yom Kippur. Ironically, that night is what congregants would have considered the holiest night of the year. The cyclone produced the strongest consistent winds that had ever been recorded. Storm surges of nearly fifteen feet were reported. Many residents were not familiar with hurricanes. So when a lull in the storm came, they ventured outside. It was at this time that the hurricane claimed many casualties. Most buildings in downtown Miami were badly damaged or entirely destroyed.

After World War II, the surging population necessitated a larger place of worship. In 1949, Beth David bought its current site on Coral Way and 26th Street.

Through the decades, the congregation experienced peaks and valleys in its membership. In the 1990s and early 2000s, its downtown location was proving a liability, as many were moving to the suburbs. Many did not frequent the downtown area. Yet, in the past decade, this has turned around. Demographic studies of Jewish Miami conducted in 2014 show a resurgence of downtown activity. This has brought more congregants to Beth David. Many are young families, and Beth David's programming is focused accordingly. It offers an early childhood center and Jewish day school. The school has a unique feature: the only autism-specific program within a Jewish day school in Florida.

Another distinguishing feature is the Beck Museum of Judaica, displaying more than five hundred Jewish artifacts. The artifacts are elegantly displayed. Italian artist Enzo Gallo designed twelve prodigious bronze panels for the doors to symbolize the twelve tribes of Israel. On both sides of the museum are large wooden reliefs made of Honduran mahogany. Artifacts are both Sephardic and Ashkenazi. Many depict lifecycle events and arts.

The Spector Ballroom is named for Samuel "Pop" Spector, a member from the original building. Spector did more than cut a check—he physically built the room. He and his sons constructed this addition in 1960. It is said that "this dedication and donation was Sam's way of expressing his love for Beth David."[6]

The Falk Sanctuary has a Bimah made out of Brazilian mahogany, adorned by trees of life on each side and ornate lighting fixtures hanging from the ceiling.

The temple offers bi-monthly Shabbats in Spanish or Portuguese. After the service, congregants partake in Argentinian or Brazilian food, drinks, music, and dancing. Melody Torrens, executive vice president of Temple David, explains how this custom began. "Many parents of students in our school are from Brazil or Argentina. We wanted them to feel relevant at our services. We decided to have the d'vor Torah (explanations of the Torah portion) in Portuguese or Spanish. This builds a sense of community and bridges Anglo and Latin families."[7]

Temple Israel
137 NE 19th Street
Phone: (305) 573-5900
Website: www.templeisrael.net

As noted earlier in this chapter, Temple Israel's history was related to that of Beth David. In 1912, Beth David (then called B'nai Zion) became the first congregation in Miami. By 1922, a schism among members over ritual and observance levels ensued. Eventually, the congregation split into the Conservative Beth David and a separate Reform congregation.

The decision of what to name the new congregation fell to donor and early member Philip Ullendorff. He decided to name it after his father.

Formed in 1922, Miami's first Reform congregation was built on what is now Biscayne Boulevard and Northeast 13th Street. The era of the 1920s was about fast moving real estate, speculation, and rampant building. Temple Israel, with its 216 member families, participated in this boom in erecting a new synagogue at its current location. Rabbi Jacob Kaplan emerged as a key early leader of the budding congregation. He was hired in 1927 and remained a member for decades until his death.

Salo Stein served as the young Temple Israel's spiritual leader.

But it was short-lived. By August 1923, he was asked to resign due to his former association with Temple Beth David. Yet Stein remained active in a less official role.

One of the first to-dos of the new congregation was to secure burial grounds for its members. So they purchased lots in the Woodlawn Cemetery.

One of the most enduring figures was Rabbi Joseph Narot. He served as rabbi for the thriving congregation from 1950 until 1980. During the turbulence of the 1960s and 1970s, Narot spoke out for civil rights. That was a difficult position when anti-civil rights actions were gripping the South. He also was against the war in the Vietnam. He met with high profile cultural icons of the time such as famed poet Allen Ginsberg.

The temple spearheaded interracial and interethnic dialogues. It hosted the first interfaith meetings of Christian, Jewish, white, and African American religious leaders at a time when that was not fashionable. The first local Head Start program started at this congregation. The thriving congregation held highly attended High Holy Day services at the Miami Beach Convention Center.

Above and opposite: One of the oldest congregations in Miami, Temple Israel is noted for its unique architecture, including brilliant light streams through the stained glass, its many mini windows of stained glass, and unique exterior wall structures. (Photos by Grace Elder.)

But in the late 1960s and 1970s, the demographics of Miami were changing. Congregants were moving to the new, spacious suburbs. Cars proliferated. Tastes changed in favor of easy parking, big lawns, and safe neighborhoods. Suddenly, the congregation's attendance began to suffer. The temple's leadership toyed with the idea of moving to Miami's suburbs themselves, but ultimately the move was not made.

In 1972, the University of Miami published *Temple Israel of Greater Miami: 1922-1972* in celebration of its fiftieth anniversary. The book celebrated the temple's history and culture. But nagging questions persisted. What was the temple's future?

The congregation was caught in a bind. On the one hand, staying in the city meant a marked attendance decrease. It dropped at one point to just four hundred families. On the other hand, moving to the suburbs felt to many like abandoning the city in its darker hours—the city that had given birth to the congregation many decades prior.

The temple emphasized its dedication to the city. In 1980, the same year the Mariel boat lifts from Cuba brought twenty-five thousand refugees to Florida, the president of the congregation, Peter Bermont, explained the temple's philosophy: "The inner city is the place we are. And we are what we are because of the inner city. We draw from so many constituencies. Our strength is that we have the ability to take from different areas. And, as downtown redevelops, we become the focal point of religious life."[8]

The president's words proved true. If history is an indicator, the decision to stay downtown has paid off. Today, the location is an asset with its proximity to the Design District and other fashionable neighborhoods Families have returned to the city. The historic congregation is once again thriving.

The architecture of the temple is striking. The history of the reverential and magnificent Gumenick Chapel is an interesting one. It is the "story of the integration of Jewish ceremonial art and architecture." The artist stated his ultimate goal was to "not only create something beautiful, but also to lift subtly the spirits of those who experience his art."[9] The chapel did not merely fill space; it re-created it. With permission from the City of Miami, it replaced the asphalt street with a terrazzo urban plaza lined with matching shade trees.

A unique Torah stand in harmony with the chapel's aesthetics. (Photo by Aaron Davidson.)

The chapel was dedicated in 1969 and took $500,000 to build. It is made to inspire. Kenneth Treister's book, *Chapel of Light*, describes the intended experience. "Upon entering the Chapel, one is overwhelmed by the absolute silence, a quietness that mysteriously reveals 4,000 years of Jewish history. The experience is similar to that sensed upon entering a Gothic cathedral. The stone seems to blossom into an organic living spirit, its noble waves heaving and swelling. The brilliant light streams through the stained glass, the shafts of sunlight infusing the air with life, symbolizing the spirituality felt in one's inner soul. It is the song Gothic architects taught us to sing."[10]

The many mini windows of stained glass, the copper menorah, the rods of golden glass stalactites, the Echad window on the eastern wall, the chandelier of copper flowers, and the two cherubim structures soaring to the flame of the eternal light are some of its unique elements. Details delight the eye. The bimah rails are curvy and decorative. The detail of the ark is subtle yet powerful. The chapel as a whole defines aesthetic unity.

Tips for the Traveler: I strongly recommend visiting the main chapel. It is breathtakingly beautiful. The temple also features prominent guest speakers (check the website). Services are open to the public.

To learn more about this historic temple, I recommend two books. *Chapel of Light: Jewish Ceremonial Art in the Sophie and Nathan Gumenick Chapel* is about the building and philosophy of the chapel. It has exquisite pictures of its architectural and decorative elements. *Temple Israel of Greater Miami: 1922-1972* details the history of the congregation during its first fifty years.

Ask also about the displays of photos and relics from the temple's and city's past. One interesting item is a Yiddish typewriter.

A Yiddish typewriter on display at Temple Israel. (Photo by Aaron Davidson.)

Cemeteries

City of Miami Cemetery
1800 NE 2nd Avenue
Phone: (305) 579-6938
Website: www.miamigov.com/parks/cemetery.html

In the rural beginnings of Miami, William Brickell's wife sold a ten-acre piece of land to the young city for $750. The location was in the country. An elderly black man was buried there in 1897, though the event was not recorded. Just a week later, the untimely death of twenty-three-year-old English H. Graham Branscomb was recorded, as was his burial. The cemetery was segregated—whites on the east end and blacks on the west end.

By 1915, the early congregation of Temple David realized it needed a burial ground. Thus marked the founding of the City of Miami Jewish section in that year. The first internment was for Morris Sack in 1915. Paul George, professor of history at Miami-Dade College, notes that "most of the burials for the Jewish section occurred up through the late 1930s, with the last Jewish burial taking place in 1964."[11]

This walled-off section is denoted by the gate displaying a Star of David and Hebrew lettering on tombstones. Until the 1950s,

Saul Cohen's kosher deli in Hotel Astley at 247 West Flagler Street in downtown Miami. (From the collections of the Jewish Museum of Florida-FIU, originated by Marcia Jo Zerivitz, founding executive director.)

this cemetery was located near Shenandoah, a vibrant Jewish community. Starting in the 1960s, Jews largely moved north of Shenandoah and gave rise to other cemeteries like Mt. Nebo Kendall Memorial Gardens.

There are other interesting sections with historical significance to visit as well. There is a memorial to the Confederate Dead put by the United Daughters of the Confederacy. Sixty-six Confederates are buried there. They are joined by their former adversaries—twenty-seven Union soldiers.

Julia Tuttle, the "Mother of Miami," is also interred in the cemetery. Born Julia DeForest Sturtevant, she was an American businesswoman who owned the land on which Miami was built. You could say she was Miami's original landlord. Tuttle is considered one of the only women founders of a major US city. A statue of her stands in Bayfront Park. She died greatly in debt, though, and has been largely forgotten, as her descendants sold off her land to pay off her debt.

Historically Jewish Neighborhoods
Shenandoah and Riverside

Riverside and Shenandoah were largely Jewish middle-class areas from the 1920s to the late 1950s. Located not far from downtown and in what is today Little Havana, these old neighborhoods still have sites worth visiting. This section concentrates on these neighborhoods and their downtown areas; the proceeding section looks at venues worth visiting in today's neighborhood of Little Havana.

Riverside was named for the nearby Miami River. Early homes were "elegant, two-story frame homes and other simpler residences with later homes bearing the bungalow style of architecture."[12] The budding neighborhood had many firsts in the area, including the first junior high, hospital, and movie theater. Its retail center was along the brimming West Flagler Street. Its parks and churches attracted residents. But it also had a dark side. The Riverside Mercantile Building served as headquarters for the Ku Klux Klan. That organization saw a revival in the 1920s in part from films like *Birth of a Nation*.

In the 1930s, the adjacent neighborhood of Shenandoah sprouted. Named for an area in Virginia, it was known for its Mediterranean revival homes. The style was popular throughout the region at the time. Later, houses were built in the streamline moderne style. The area's commercial district was along Southwest 8th Street and Coral Way.

By the late 1950s, an urban exodus took place as many residents moved to the suburbs. During the 1950s, years before Fidel Castro took power in Cuba, many Cuban refugees resided in this area. Paul George, a professor at Miami-Dade College and author of books on the region, notes that a network and support system was set up before the period we think of as the mass Cuban immigration. Cuban Jews during this period usually moved to Miami Beach rather than to Shenandoah, as there were stronger Jewish networks there. That said, some Cuban Jews lamented the cold welcome that often greeted arrivals in Miami Beach.

Notable people, transportation, and places (some still existing and others torn down) include the following:

- In 1925, a trolley line ran along West Flagler Street in the heart of downtown through Riverside. Another line ran through Coral Way and downtown through Shenandoah. It operated until the mid-1930s.
- The Cowen family, early Jewish residents of Riverside, operated a successful downtown shoe business.
- Donald Lavigne Uniforms produced military attire for the armed forces.
- In the 1920s at 1535 Southwest 3rd Street stood a former Jewish Orthodox synagogue, the first in the Riverside neighborhood. Years later, the congregation Shaarei Zeddeck occupied the synagogue. Today, it is home to a Latino Jehovah's Witness church.
- At 514 Southwest 22nd Avenue stood Shenandoah's Candies, known for its coconut patties in chocolate. The specialty was fitting as the neighborhood had many coconut palm trees until a significant portion died from a disease in the 1970s. The establishment opened in the early 1930s and serviced a national clientele through mail orders.
- At 6th Avenue and Flagler Street stood Robert's Drugs with its unique signage. Open all night, it served lunch and filled prescriptions. It closed in the 1990s.

- At 1310 West Flagler Street was neighborhood favorite Cushman Bakery, owned by Robert Wolfarth. Delivery trucks brought goodies to homes throughout the area. From the bakery to city hall, Wolfarth later became the mayor of Miami.
- Early pioneer Isidor Cohen's wife, Ida, help found Miami Jewish Home. In the 1940s, it became the Miami Jewish Home and Hospital for the Aged at Southwest Fourth Street and 12th Avenue.
- At West Flagler and Northwest 12th Avenue was Tyler's Restaurant, known for its "power lunches."
- At 29 West Flagler Street was the Dade County Auditorium, which housed services for Jewish High Holidays.
- Temple Beth El at 500 Southwest 17th Avenue was one of the largest and oldest synagogues in the area.
- At 1101 Southwest 12th Avenue, Miami Jewish Congregation opened its doors in the late 1940s. It became the Miami Hebrew School and Junior Congregation and then, years later, the Beth Kodesh Synagogue. Now it is a Latino Baptist Church. Look carefully at the cross above the front entrance and you will see faint traces of the Start of David that once adorned the synagogue.

Stroll around the downtown area, once home to early Jewish merchants and establishments. Start at North Miami Avenue and Flagler Street. Here, Flagler divides east and west and Miami Avenue north and south. Macy's stands here at the former site of the prominent department store Burdine's. The store dates back to 1896 as a carriage trade shop for the sparse population in Bartow, Florida. In 1898, Burdine purchased this block and opened the store to capitalize on increased demand from the new railroad. Later, it became a well-known chain replete with tropical colors and themes. Decades later, it became Macy's.

The owner subsidized Isidor Cohen's self-published autobiography, *Historical Sketches and Sidelights of Miami, Florida* in 1925.

Walk south on South Miami Avenue to Southeast 2nd Street. This was where early Jewish pioneer Isidor Cohen sold men's clothing. His store was considered successful and competed with larger department stores. Later, he moved a few blocks north and entered the real estate business. Cohen was not only a merchant, real estate professional, and author but also a founder of many Jewish and civic organizations. In 1900, he was one of three Jews in Miami. The two others were his friend and business partner Jake

Schneidman and his wife, Ida Schneidman. Jake died soon after, though, and Isidor married the widowed Ida. Other early Jewish merchants in the area included Sam Singer, Julius Frank, and Morris Kanner. Isidor Cohen is buried in Mount Nebo Cemetery.

Walk back up to Flagler and you can imagine the commerce from early decades in the twentieth century. These include a shoe store, Grand's Bakery, and Rosedale Deli (one of the first delis in the area), among many other establishments. Rosedale Deli closed in the 1970s, but oldtimers recall its legendary lamb shank. David Afremow established the New York Bargain Store in 1909. Later, the business became Cromer and Cassel and then Richard's Department Store. Beth David, the area's first temple, was named after David Afremow. Also nearby was the clothing and supply chain store the Hub, owned by the Rubin family.

Mitchell Wolfson, a prominent business owner, moved to Miami from Key West. He developed movie theaters and tourist attractions to the area.

Little Havana

In the 1930s, Little Havana was a thriving lower-middle-class Jewish neighborhood marked by Riverside and Shenandoah. By the 1940s, many Jews left the neighborhood for the new suburbs or for Miami Beach. By the early 1960s, it transitioned to a largely Cuban neighborhood with many residents who fled Castro's Cuba. It became a social and cultural center for the Cuban exile community. By the late 1970s and 1980s, many of these Cuban immigrants moved away to more affluent areas. New immigrants from Cuba and other Latin American countries replaced them. During this period, the neighborhood fell into urban decay. Streets were dirty and crime-filled. Yet in the late 1990s the neighborhood changed yet again. Gentrification in Miami improved the neighborhood. Today, Latinos from diverse countries like Nicaragua and Honduras have joined the neighborhood. It boasts several cultural attractions and festivals. Still, its heritage is also threatened by rampant development.

Stroll through this unique neighborhood. Gaze at the colorful murals, visit the monuments to its heroes, listen to Cuban jazz, and watch a competitive game of dominoes at Domino Park. Do it all with the energy you will feel from the Cuban coffee sold on almost every corner.

The neighborhood is known for its Cuban restaurants, live music, monuments, and cigar shops. Southwest 8th Street, or Calle Ocho, is the hub.

A *National Geographic* article describes the scene. "The repetitive, rump-shaking beats of salsa and merengue pour out of storefronts and restaurants, sometimes joined by the staccato crowing of a rooster in a neighboring backyard. The street is lined with coffee counters, beauty salons, and barber shops, little food markets, art galleries, dollar stores, *botanicas* filled with candles and statues that are part of the Santeria Afro-Caribbean religion, cafes, Cuban nostalgia shops, and bakeries offering racks of crusty Cuban bread and guava pastries."[13]

Today, as Miami gentrifies, the future of the neighborhood's cultural and historic preservation is in doubt. Developers are purchasing properties at a fast rate and building new homes. It is a subject of controversy. National Public Radio ran a segment on the show *All Things Considered* exploring this issue. Some residents lamented losing the authenticity of the neighborhood. For instance, one resident interviewed on the show worried that "with the plans that are being pushed, you are going to end up with a modern box building next to a 1920s bungalow."[14] Yet others noted that skyscrapers will not be built and that the neighborhood is deteriorating and is in need of changes. Still, the National Trust for Historic Preservation has placed the neighborhood on a list of Most Endangered Historic Places.

In some ways, Little Havana's history parallels that of New York's Harlem. During the late nineteenth and early twentieth centuries, Harlem was a center of Jewish life. In the 1920s, many Jews moved out to other areas of New York. Large numbers of African Americans, many of whom migrated from the South, moved in. Harlem's Golden Age was born. Jazz clubs like the Cotton Club were thriving. But after the Great Depression of the 1930s and World War II, the neighborhood fell into a sharp decline. Poverty and crime were rampant for decades. Finally, in the 2000s, the forsaken neighborhood began to gentrify. Today, like that of Little Havana, its ethnic heritage is threatened by massive development of the neighborhood, which is now seen as prime real estate. Learn more about the history of Jewish Harlem in *Jewish New York: A History and Guide to Neighborhoods, Synagogues, and Eateries.*

Tips for the Traveler: On the last Friday of each month, you can catch Viernes Culturales (Cultural Fridays). There are sometimes outdoor musical performances, cuisine tastings, films, art gallery openings, and more. You can take a tour of the neighborhood, offered most days.

If you explore on your own, start your journey on Calle Ocho. Watch the scenes of daily life, like residents playing dominoes. Smell the aroma of Cuban coffee. Sample the food and try one of the local coconut milks.

Look down and you'll see the Little Havana version of the Hollywood Walk of Fame. On 8th Street from 12th to 17th Avenues, the star-studded plaques line the street. Probably one of the most famous to a mainstream audience is Gloria Estefan. See how many you know.

Visit the four-block boulevard just off Calle Ocho and see the various monuments dedicated to Cuban freedom fighters. It's a glimpse into Cuban history. Many concern the controversial 1961 Bay of Pigs invasion. Others are tributes to Cuban journalists who bravely wrote stories against the Cuban regime.

Watch retirees play competitive domino games throughout the day at Domino Park. Look to the side and you will see murals of world leaders who came to the area for the first Summit of the Americas in 1994. The park itself is also called Maximo Gomez Park after a Cuban fighter against the Spanish at the turn of the twentieth century.

Next door is the Tower Theater, built in 1926. Its architecture is classic art deco style. The theater was a popular place to watch matinees. Once the area became a center for Cuban refugees, it was among the few cinemas to add Spanish subtitles. Today, it's an art-house cinema operated by Miami-Dade College.

If you're interested in the Bay of Pigs event, visit the Bay of Pigs Museum. It carries pictures, flags, and memorabilia of Cuban soldiers of the Assault Brigade 2506, which invaded Cuba on

Retirees play domino games at Maximo Gomez Park, affectionately referred to as Domino Park. (Photo by Aaron Davidson.)

April 17, 1961. Most died at the Bay of Pigs. Some believe anti-Castro dissidents along with rogue elements within the Central Intelligence Agency in partnership with the mafia were behind the assassination of John F. Kennedy. Others insist it was carried out by a lone gunman, Lee Harvey Oswald. Over a half-century later, Kennedy's assassination is still controversial.

Looking to spruce up your outfit? Try Alfaro's Boutique, which sells linen guayaberas for men and guayabera-style dresses, pants, and suits for women. You'll feel the local flavor and service with a seamstress dutifully working at a sewing machine in the back of the store ready to fit your purchase for you. Once you have been fitted, enjoy Alfrao's Restaurant next door. It's known for its live music.

If you're curious about cigars, one of Cuba's most famous exports, stop into the Maxoly Cuban Cigar Gallery. Other cigar stores are also open nearby. The smell of the various cigar flavors fills the room. Watch the men roll up the cigars in the front.

Famous Ball and Chain Bar and Lounge in 1935. In its early decades, it achieved notoriety from gambling, liquor law violations, and associations with gangsters. It was among the first music spots to integrate black and white performers. Today, it is an integral part of Little Havana.

Other Museums and Cultural Attractions

These venues do not have a direct Jewish connection. However, they are very important in the culture and history of Miami.

HistoryMiami Museum
101 W Flagler Street
Phone: (305) 375-1492
Website: www.historymiami.org
Hours: Mon.–Sat., 10 a.m.–5 p.m.; Sun., 12 p.m.-5 p.m.
Admission: Adults $10

If you like history, definitely consider a visit to HistoryMiami. It's located on a plaza near downtown with a research library, a former art museum, and a documentation collection. The history museum puts in perspective the long history of the region. It showcases artifacts from the pre-Columbus era—such as boats, tools, and early musical instruments—and then puts in perspective how Miami came about as a world-class city. Make sure to view the films. Some are shown in naturalized settings like huts that early inhabitants would have used.

The museum has Smithsonian Institution accreditation, which allows it to bring Smithsonian exhibits to the area.

Make sure to visit the photo collections, which rotate on various topics. Some have dealt with photojournalism and the capturing of crucial moments in recent history, like the refugees on the Mariel boat lifts from Cuba.

The research center, open only on weekdays by appointment, offers digital photo archives of Southeast Florida and the Caribbean from 1883 to the present, as well as historic maps, a photo store, and photo essays that are "curated selections of pictures from collections with each exploring a different topic."[15] There are also oral history tapes and transcripts of individuals from the area. Another collection specializes in architectural records.

The museum offers a unique program called Miami Stories in which Miami-Dade County residents can share their "unique Miami-related experiences." The program was created to "collect, preserve and disseminate personal accounts of these experiences as a way to illuminate the past and enlighten the future."[16]

Also consider a tour of the area on land or by boat. Check the museum's website for more information.

Vizcaya Museum and Gardens
3251 S Miami Avenue
Phone: (305) 250-9133
Website: www.vizcaya.org
Hours: 9:30 a.m.–4:30 p.m.; Tues., closed
Admission: Adults $18

One of Miami's most famous historic houses, Vizcaya was the opulent winter home of the industrialist James Deering. Not well known, Deering made his fortune from Deering Harvester, a manufacturer of agricultural machinery and construction equipment. Famed investment banker J. P. Morgan merged Deering's company with others to form the conglomerate International Harvester.

As you approach you the mansion on its sprawling grounds, you may think you are in Italy. Though built in 1914, it is made to look much older, and to look European. It is in the Mediterranean revival architecture style with Baroque elements. The estate includes Italian-style Renaissance gardens and a landscape of native plants.

The house in many ways typifies the end of the Gilded Age. This was a time of vast income differences between the rich and poor. Often, the super-rich paid very little income tax. Building ornately decorated mansions was in vogue. This trend can be seen in other houses discussed in this book that were also built around this time.

Though hard to imagine today, the site was mangrove swamps in the early twentieth century. Deering had an interest in conservation and wanted to minimize destruction to the forests adjacent to the property.

In 1914, construction started. Perhaps the best way to summarize the concept is to describe it as an Italian Renaissance aesthetic with a South Florida tropical flavor. The gardens, for example, used French and Italian layouts, yet the plentiful mineral of limestone was used along with tropical plants.

Deering moved into this winter residence on Christmas Day 1916. His friends marked the day with lavish celebrations and strangely dressed in Italian peasant costumes.

Deering lived in the house alone but often entertained. Pres. Warren Harding was one visitor. A silent-film buff, Deering enjoyed screening Hollywood films in the courtyard of the main house. He hired art curators to collect the extensive antiquities present in the house. He spent winters there until his death at the age of sixty-six.

As was common with such estates during this period, a large staff lived on or near the property. Some tended the house, while others worked in the gardens.

Why the name Vizcaya? Deering had a fascination with Europe and explorers. Vizcaya references a northern province in Spain of the same name that is located in the Basque region along the Atlantic's Bay of Biscay. So too did Vizcaya face the Biscayne Bay. Another explanation for the name was Deering's interest in the Spanish explorer Sebastian Vizcaino, who may have explored Florida.

Sadly, Deering died in 1925 while aboard the steamship SS

City of Paris. His was single and bequeathed his estate to his two nieces.

The inheritance turned out to be a mixed blessing. The hurricane of 1926, just a year after Deering's death, devastated the property. Maintenance costs were astronomical, so Deering's nieces decided to sell portions to the Catholic Diocese of St. Augustine. By the 1950s, Miami-Dade County bought the villa and gardens and extensively renovated them. It became the Dade County Art Museum.

In 1998, the property became governed by the Vizcaya Museum and Gardens Trust.

The villa has more than seventy rooms. Many are decorated with antiques dating from the fifteenth century to the nineteenth century.

Vizcaya has hosted world leaders over the decades. Pres. Ronald Reagan met with Pope John Paul II here during the pope's initial visit to South Florida.

Tips for the Traveler: I recommend a tour of the house. It covers only the first floor, but it explains the varied interior decorative styles, antiques, and life of John Deering.

After the tour, explore the second floor on your own. Look for windy staircases in back rooms leading to little-explored, almost hidden rooms.

I also highly recommend the night tours of the garden offered during the winter months. You can pretend it's the early twentieth century and that you are a guest of Mr. Deering. Wine and hors d'oeuvres at the café will make it more fun. Tours run through the evening. The price is $20, but tickets are available.

Another tip is to try the café. It also offers high tea on Sundays. You can also take Prana Yoga classes on the lawn on select Sundays.

If you would like to learn more about Vizcaya or take a home a souvenir, you can watch the 2009 PBS documentary on the estate's history called *Vizcaya: Palace of Dreams.* It was produced by PBS member station WPBT2 in Miami.

Deering Estate at Cutler
16701 SW 72nd Avenue
Phone: (305) 235-1668
Website: www.deeringestate.org
Hours: 10 a.m. to 5 p.m. (no admission after 4 p.m.)
Admission: Adults $12

The Deering Estate at Cutler has origins similar to Vizcaya.

It is a combination of a historic house, land to explore, and a cultural arts center. A lesser-known aspect is what lies beneath this storied estate. Pre-historic human fossils and tools were discovered on the land. Some are on now on exhibit for visitors.

Charles Deering lived on the property from 1922 until his death in 1927. This coincided with the winter residence of his brother, James Deering, at Vizcaya from 1922-1924.

The house dates to 1900, when Miami was sparsely populated. It served as an inn and housed guests like Henry Flagler, the father of the railroad in Florida.

Deering purchased the house in 1916 and moved in six years later. He only ended up living there for five years, dying just two years after his brother, James. Both brothers made their fortunes from the agricultural equipment business and the conglomerate of International Harvester.

The estate contains the Cutler Burial Mound, including artifacts that date back to the Belle Glades II and III periods—defined roughly as 200-700 AD and 700-1300 AD. It is believed that the mound is the burial site of twelve to eighteen Native Americans.

After Deering's death, the estate was willed to his wife and children. In subsequent decades, it became public. It is part of the Miami-Dade County Parks, Recreation, and Open Space Department. This organization oversees the estate on behalf of the State of Florida.

In August 1992, Hurricane Andrew ravaged the Deering property. Waves reached as high as the second floor of the building and caused severe flooding. It took several years for the estate to be fully reopened to the public.

Tips for the Traveler: Besides the historic house, the estate offers a lot of unique arts performances. Mr. Deering enjoyed collecting and supporting the arts. In his legacy, the estate offers many artistic ventures.

The Artist Village offers plays, arts, and music. Some concerts focus on iconic American composers such as Aaron Copland. Other concerts feature classic music like Bach or contemporary groups like the French pop duo Daft Punk, the recipient of several Grammy awards in recent years.

Some concerts are outside, so bring blankets or lawn chairs. It's a perfect setting for a picnic.

There is also a free exhibit during the evenings that showcases various artistic displays. Most events are free. In many, the public can interact with artists.

If you like theater, try the One-Minute Play Festival. It's a dizzying array of one-minute plays from about thirty local playwrights. According to the festival, "the work attempts to reflect the theatrical landscape of local artistic communities by creating a dialogue between the collective conscious and the individual voice through a performance of many moments and includes responses to local topics such as immigration, government and culture."[17] Learn more at www.oneminuteplayfestival.com.

Beside these general festivals, other events focus on particular composers. Are you a fan of Franz Liszt? A local series plays concerts at the Deering Estate, among other local venues.

In additional, there is the supernatural part of the Deering Estate. Some say the site has been home to paranormal activity. The property is near a prehistoric burial mound.

The estate offers "spook-overs" and ghost tours. According to a *Miami Herald* article, the Deering Estate's staff "claimed to notice abnormal occurrences for years, and invited the League of Paranormal Investigations to lead monthly explorations."[18]

The staff notes they have voice recordings and pictures of apparitions. The spook-overs are typically from 11 p.m. to 4 a.m. Skeptics are welcome.

Miami Design District

This is a prime shopping district for fashion, luxury, and art. The neighborhood embodies urban renewal. For decades, it was known as Buena Vista. During Miami's downturn, it was deteriorating, and crime was a problem. The neighborhood did not revitalize until the early 2000s. Both public and private funds were contributed. The aesthetics of the neighborhood were reset as streets and sidewalks were beautified.

Some credit Craig Robbins for the turnaround. He bought up run-down buildings and influenced key designers and artists to relocate to the area. The district followed the rough trajectory of SoHo in New York in that respect.

Today, luxury stores punctuate its streets. True to its name, design and art galleries are spread throughout the Northeast 2nd Avenue area.

Miami's Design District is pedestrian friendly. Enjoy a stroll through the neighborhood's many shops, galleries, restaurants, and design installations.

Coconut Grove

Nestled on the shores near the Biscayne Bay sits one of the oldest neighborhoods in Miami: Coconut Grove. Nineteenth-century mariners knew it as a favorite stop. Early residents referred to the area as Coconut Grove because of the nearby coconut trees.

Early residents opened a guest house for visitors or sailors. That became the Bay View Inn, which served as the first hotel in the area. This also shifted the local demographics. Black Bahamians settled the region, since many worked in the inn.

The area gradually developed a reputation for writers, naturalists, and artists. Many of these guests of the inn decided to stay in the area. Thus began its Bohemian reputation.

The quiet early days ended with the 1896 introduction of Henry Flagler's Florida East Coast Railway. (See chapter one for more information.)

Subsequent decades saw more artists move into the area. By the late 1960s, it was part of the counterculture. Today, Coconut Grove is the home of festivals.

Tips for the Traveler: Stroll through the village center and explore the art galleries, small cafes, and local stores. Consider a visit to the Barnacle Historic State Park, which has the oldest house in Miami-Dade County.

Check to see when the next Junkanoo Festival, also called the Goombay Festival, is being held. Along Grand Avenue are various family-friendly activities and pieces related to traditional Bahamian folklore with a nod to the region's ethnic past.

The following are some other sites to browse in Coconut Grove:

Peacock Park (2820 McFarlane Road): The park is the home of the first hotel in the area, the Bay View Inn. It was a gathering place of early entrepreneurs, writers, and artists.

Coconut Grove Library (2875 McFarlane Road): This was the site of the Pine Needles, a club for young girls in 1895 when Miami was first developed. It became one of the first libraries in the area. Just left of the library entrance is Miami's oldest grave (1882). It belongs to early pioneer and environmentalist Ralph Munroe's first wife, Eva Hewitt Munroe.

Old Bank of Coconut Grove (3430 Main Highway): This building housed the Bank of Coconut Grove. Later, it was the center for something special: interspecies communication between humans and dolphins.

Coconut Grove Playhouse (3500 Main Highway): The playhouse was established as a movie theater in 1927, a year when cinema was forever changed with *The Jazz Singer*, the first talkie. Silent films were in decline. Decades later, a wealthy developer purchased it and renovated it as a theater.

Historic Synagogues

There are also some nearby synagogues. Temple Judea was founded in 1948 in nearby Coral Gables as the Coral Gables Jewish Center. An exhibit on Temple Judea's history at the Coral Gables Museum described its journey from a congregation of a few families to the current one of six hundred families. It showcased ritual and historic objects as well as pictures of multi-generational members. A timeline on the wall outlined major developments over the past decades. You can still catch a glimpse of the exhibit on a news segment through YouTube. Inquire at the temple if you would like to learn more.

Eateries

These eateries offer Jewish-style deli fare, Israeli and Middle Eastern food, or Kosher meals in Miami and its surrounding suburbs.

Miami

The Daily Creative Food Company
2001 Biscayne Boulevard #109
Phone: (305) 573-4535
Website: www.thedailyfood.com

"New York City in the heart of downtown Miami," proclaims this unique eatery. It is a themed establishment where you can read comics or newspaper headlines by glancing at the walls. The informal venue offers breakfast, soups, paninis, and many kinds of sandwiches.

Etzel Itzik Deli
18757 W Dixie Highway
Phone: (305) 937-1546
Website: www.etzelitzik.com

Israeli cuisine prevails at this informal venue. Try the Moroccan fish, goulash, eggplant with tomato sauce, and vegetarian kubbe. The meats are kosher.

Roasters and Toasters
18515 NE 18th Avenue
Phone: (305) 830-3354
Website: www.miamiroastersntoasters.com

Opened in 1984, this classic deli with iconic photos on the walls offers much of the classic deli fare once prominent in the area.

Its name derives from its origins as a coffee shop that roasted its own beans. Al and Sandy Burger came up with an idea that they would eventually have patented: a bagel ball.

By the mid-1990s, the enterprising couple sold the coffee shop to Jack Kantrowitz and Dan Kaplan. They saw an opportunity to turn the fledgling coffee house into a deli, which proved successful.

Jack Kantrowitz died in a tragic motorcycle accident. Five years later, the restaurant endured a major fire. However, it persevered and today continues to offer classic deli fare.

Other locations mentioned in this book are in Miami Beach and in a casino near Fort Lauderdale.

Subres Grill
2218 NE 123rd Street
Phone: (305) 899-0095
Website: www.subresgrill.com

Try Subres Grill for kosher Middle Eastern and Mediterranean cuisines. They also offer vegetarian options like Israeli-style salads with hummus. Popular deserts include strudel and chocolate soufflé served with ice cream. Opened in January 2013, Subres Grill is owned by an Israeli couple, Eli and Etty Weinberg. It's in a lively Jewish neighborhood in North Miami and features contemporary décor.

Hallandale Beach

Sage Bagel and Appetizer Shop
800 E Hallandale Beach Boulevard
Phone: (954) 456-7499
Website: www.sagebagelanddeli.com

In 1972, Milton and Iris Fuerst began this informal bagel-baking operation, leaving the quick pace of Queens behind. The store was small and focused on bagels and simple appetizers. Today, it's a full-service deli and restaurant. The restaurant prides itself on making almost everything from scratch, eschewing mixes and fillers.

Brickell

Toasted Bagelry and Deli
83 SW 8th Street
Phone: (305) 400-6996
Website: www.toastedbagelry.com

This informal classic bagelry wins high marks from customers for its fresh bagels and menu of Miami-named sandwiches. One writer humorously describes the long lines. "Do the math: 800 billion trillion condo units going up in Brickell. One deli. This explains why the wait here on a weekend is only slightly shorter than the wait to get on I-95 at 5:30 p.m."[19]

Chapter Four

Broward County

Broward County has one of the largest concentrations of Jews in Florida. The county includes about thirty cities; perhaps the best known are Fort Lauderdale, Deerfield Beach, Hallandale Beach, Plantation, and Weston.

One of the earliest Jews in the area, Louis Brown, arrived in Dania in 1910. By 1923, seven Jewish families resided in Fort Lauderdale, including Mack and Moe Katz, who came to speculate in real estate. It is believed that Moe held one of the state's first real estate licenses. The lure of the real estate boom brought many other Jews in the mid-1920s. Early Jews often specialized in retail in downtown Fort Lauderdale. One example is Sterling's Men and Boys Store.

The budding community founded its first congregation on Las Olas Boulevard. But fortunes turned with the Great Hurricane of 1926, which destroyed newly built homes and businesses. By the late 1930s, the area was economically blossoming again, spurred by increased tourism and residential construction.

Hollywood grew into a major city in Broward County. Sam Horvitz, a Jewish real estate developer, built many single-family homes, residential communities, and malls.

Jews in the rural parts of the county worked in agriculture growing crops like tomatoes, cucumbers, and citrus and harvesting dairy products.

Russian-born Morris Cooper immigrated to the United States near the turn of the twentieth century. Penniless, he toiled in a shirt factory. Within a few decades, though, he created Cooper City.

In 1966, the first Jewish mayor in Broward County was elected in Hollywood. In the 1970s and 1980s, an important population shift among Jews occurred. Jewish retirees were moving to Broward rather than to Miami-Dade County. Part of this shift was fueled by increased crime during the period in Miami and Miami Beach. By the 1990s, there were about 275,000 Jews in Broward County, including many elderly—the median age of the Jewish population was fifty-nine. About 10 percent were snowbirds, residents of northeastern states living in the county for the winter. Latino, Israeli, and Russian Jews moved to the area, as did a significant number of Holocaust survivors.

Yet over the last decade, the Jewish population of Broward County has declined. Many of the elderly have passed away and have not been replaced by new retirees, who instead have chosen the suburbs of southern Palm Beach County.

Today, you can explore the old Jewish community in downtown Fort Lauderdale and visit historic synagogues like Temple Emanuel and Temple Sinai. A visit to the newly located Holocaust Documentation and Education Center is a must. Trace your family's history at the Jewish Genealogy Society of Broward County. Order pastrami on rye at some of the area's many New York-style delis.

Historic Houses and Museums
Dania Beach

Holocaust Documentation and Education Center
303 N Federal Highway
Phone: (954) 929-5690
Website: www.hdec.org
Check website for current hours

Founded in 1980 by the late Sister Trinita Flood of Barry University, the recently relocated Holocaust Documentation and Education Center is a must see. The center is "dedicated to documenting the authentic memory of the Holocaust and educating today's generation about the evils and dangers of hatred, bigotry, and bullying."[1]

Sister Trinita's vision was to bring together every South Florida college and university president to guide the organization. That vision of cross-organization cooperation continues today.

The museum features important reminders and relics from the Holocaust. One exhibit showcases the only identified Holocaust railcar in the world. It is a boxcar from Poland that was used to transport Jews and other prisoners to labor and death camps. It is astonishing and poignant to see. The museum acquired the railcar from the Bureau of Polish Railroad Lines in Wroclaw in 2006. For over four years, it underwent restoration to its original wartime state. In the course of renovation, "two complete sets of German identification and designation numbers were revealed on the undercarriage of the Railcar. These were both conclusively painted up the frame of the Railcar during German Railway service, confirming its use during the Second World War."[2] Also featured is a United States Sherman army tank, which tore down barbed wire and liberated death camps. Steve Gellar, the museum's chairman, notes the contrast among the two objects: "The alpha and the omega, the railcar that carried so many to hell and the tank that liberated so many people from hell."[3]

Besides a museum, the center serves as a place where survivors can teach younger generations about what happened during the Holocaust. Norman Frajman of Boynton Beach, for example, is a Holocaust survivor volunteering with the center. He explains,

A restored railcar that was used to transport victims to concentration camps during the Holocaust. At least two sets of German designation numbers on the undercarriage were revealed during restoration. (Housed at the Holocaust Documentation and Education Center.)

"Our aim is to leave a legacy for the ones whose voices have been silenced." Many contribute not only their stories but also personal artifacts. Frajman brought his brown and blue-striped shirt that was part of his uniform at Buchenwald, a labor and death camp.[4]

The center also includes "videotaping facilities to interview survivors and their children, a reference library, over 2,500 eyewitness testimonies from survivors, liberators and rescuers and 6,000 artifacts, documents and photographs."[5] Importantly, all interviewers of survivors undergo a rigorous fifty-four-hour training program. Rita Hofrichter—a survivor, former resistance fighter, and volunteer from the organization's inception—conducts the training with her expertise and unique background. All oral histories are transcribed, edited, and proofread. The goal is to have these available online through the center's digital library program.

The center is highly focused on education efforts with school-age children. Student Awareness Days provide interactions with survivors of the Holocaust to foster a dialogue with living history, and the center conducts a teacher training in the summer to assist educators in implementing the state mandate on Holocaust education. The center is also known for student contests in which

US M4A3 Sherman tank of the type that was used during the liberation of the concentration camps during the Holocaust. (On permanent display at the Holocaust Documentation and Education Center.)

students are encouraged to submit songs, videos, poems, or photographs relaying their experiences learning about this topic.

Educational outreach coordinator Stephanie Cohen notes that for some students World War II seems like abstract history. Common themes that students can relate to, like bullying, are presented.

As a nod to the community it services, the Holocaust Documentation and Education Center is the first museum in North America to tell the story of the Holocaust in English and Spanish.

Rositta Kenigsberg, president of the center, played a key role in passing the 1994 Florida law mandating Holocaust education. Today, Holocaust education is compulsory for each student in the State of Florida.

Kenigsberg makes an important point about studying crucial historical events like the Holocaust. Conventional wisdom may say that events are less important to be studied the further back they are in history; but Kenigsberg notes that the opposite is true. "In time, more is revealed and the study becomes actually more crucial. Even in recent decades, we have learned much about the events surrounding the Holocaust."[6] Another reason why study becomes increasingly important is so that future generations can learn about history once those who have lived through it have passed on.

The Holocaust Documentation and Education Center is located in a spacious 26,000 square feet building near Fort Lauderdale. Gallagher and Associates, the Maryland designers of the Museum of Jewish Heritage in New York and the National Museum of American Jewish History in Philadelphia, served as the lead designer.

Plantation

Jewish Genealogical Society of Broward County
6501 W Sunrise Boulevard (second floor of the administration building)
Phone: (754) 223-9201
Website: www.jgsbc.org

Learn about your family roots at the Jewish Genealogical Society of Broward County (JGSBC). Started in 1988, JGSBC seeks to preserve and research genealogical information and family histories.

At the heart of the facility on the campus of the Soref Jewish

Community Center is the library of research materials. It is open to all Broward County residents. Visitors can call to inquire about use. The librarians will not conduct the genealogical research for you, but they will show how to explore your family's history and provide tools to do so.

The library contains records of local Jewish cemeteries, including Evergreen Cemetery. It also contains census data dating back to 1920 and population studies of American Sephardi and Canadian Jewry.

Soref Jewish Community Center
6501 W Sunrise Boulevard
Phone: (954) 792-6700
Website: www.sorefjcc.org

The Soref Jewish Community Center is one of the oldest in the county. Started in 1977, it operates from a sixteen-acre Florida Air Academy property.

The center offers the usual children, adult, and senior programming and athletic facilities. Yet there are some unique offerings. The Alvin and Evelyn Gross My Jewish Discovery Place Children's Museum is an interactive museum of culture, history, and values. Recent exhibits include discovering an archaeological dig, picking vegetables from a kibbutz garden, singing music about the creation story, and much more.

For college students, there is the Murray I. Daninhirsch Student Loan Fund, providing interest-free loans for undergraduate study for local families. Loan maximums are $6,000.

Fort Lauderdale

Visit what was part of the old Jewish community in downtown Fort Lauderdale in the Las Olas Boulevard area, or explore some of the oldest retail establishments from Jewish pioneers around Andrews Avenue.

Las Olas Boulevard

Interlaced with canals, waterfront homes, museums, a historic hotel, and numerous eateries and galleries, Las Olas Boulevard stands as one of Fort Lauderdale's central spots. One of the earliest synagogues was located here. The area is walkable—a rarity as most places require a car even to go short distances. The commercial area is just about a mile.

Las Olas means "the waves" in Spanish, which is appropriate given the boulevard's proximity to the ocean. The area dates back to the early days of Fort Lauderdale when the population was sparse. Like most of the region, it was primarily swampy wetlands. In the 1920s, when the area was quickly being developed, the area was dredged to eventually become the commercial district. It fell into disrepair in later decades but was reconstructed in the 1980s.

There is a large Chabad center on Las Olas Boulevard that offers adult learning, weekly and Shabbat services, Hebrew school, a mikvah (ritual bath), and a Judaica gift shop. The mikvah is noted as state of the art and offers spa amenities and massages. The Judaica shop offers jewelry, books, religious items, and decorations.

Movie stars and socialites lived near this area, including a number of actors who played comic-book heroes. Residents included the original Tarzan, Johnny Weissmuller, and Lee Majors of the *Six Million Dollar Man*, who was married to Farrah Fawcett.

The earliest residents were Frank and Ivy Stranahan. They were the "father and mother" of Fort Lauderdale and had a strong bond with the Seminole Indian tribe prominent in this area. Learn more about the Stranahans on page 164.

Tips for the Traveler: Stroll down the boulevard and visit the shops, galleries, and eateries. Las Olas also has four museums:

- The Museum of Discovery and Science offers interactive exhibits on local biology, including pet alligators, iguanas, and the Everglades. Children may enjoy the Eco Discovery Center, where they can experience hurricane-force winds. There's also an IMAX movie theater.
- NSU Museum of Art Fort Lauderdale showcases more than six thousand works. Part of Nova Southeastern

University, the museum is best known for its collection
of drawings and paintings from American realist William
Glackens. It also houses the works of key mid-twentieth-
century artists like Lee Krasner (who was Jackson Pollack's
wife) and Frank Stella. There is some non-western art too,
like African, Native American, and Oceanic.
- Historic Needham Estate is not open to the public for
viewing. Unless your relative invites you to his wedding
held at this venue, you probably cannot see the inside. It
was built in 1925 at the height of the area's rapid growth
and has had various uses over the years. Once the host
to FDR and Winston Churchill, the estate later became a
modeling school and then a girls' finishing school. Current
owner Sandy Romanovitz notes that "much of the house
is original, from the wrought-iron stairway banisters,
Cuban tile floors and Pecky Cypress ceilings in the family
room to the beveled glass in the floor to ceiling doors in
the living room."[7]
- The Stranahan House is the oldest surviving structure in
Broward County. (See page 164 for more information.)

Former Site of Sterling's Men and Boys Store
218 SW 1st Avenue

Though its traces are gone today, this was the site of one of
Broward County's oldest retail stores. Bernard Sterling, an early
Jewish settler of the region, laid its foundation in the 1920s after
peddling fabric across the south from his Model T. Graduating
from peddling, Sterling opened the eponymous department store
in Perrine, a town near Miami. In 1934, he opened a Sterling's Men
and Boys store in the budding town of Fort Lauderdale in what
was a converted garage on Andrews Avenue. The store specialized
in work clothes for men. In later years, it sold sportswear apparel.

Sterling's father, Isadore "Pops" Sterling, became known for
his generosity in giving away shoes and other apparel to Florida's
needy. He was also very generous in donating to philanthropic
causes, referred to as the Jewish Santa Claus. "I give back what
has been given to me," he once said.[8]

Eventually, Bernard's uncle took over the company and opened additional stores. His family's descendants played key roles in the business in subsequent decades. In the 1970s, the store introduced the Hip Pocket idea, a blue jean specialty product modeled after a product at Gap. Soon, the enterprising family opened Hip Pocket stores.

The last store, which was on Las Olas Boulevard, closed in the 1990s. It was the end of an era. Today the building is the Florida Department of Environmental Protection.

Davie

Jewish Federation of Broward County–PJ Library
5890 S Pine Island Road
Phone: (954) 252-6900
Website: www.jewishbroward.org

They say there is no such thing as a free lunch. Apparently, that's not the case with the PJ Library gift book program. Broward families with children between six months and eight years old can receive PJ library books and music for free. The goal is to deepen families' Jewish experience and strengthen communities.

Each month, the library sends free books or CDs to recipients so they can build their libraries of Jewish literature.

Historic Temples

Plantation

Temple Emanu-El (and its merger today with Temple Kol Ami)
8200 Peters Road
Phone: (954) 472-1988
Website: http://tkae.org/

One of the oldest congregations in South Florida, Temple Emanu-El began in 1926. The founding members rented a room above a restaurant on Andrews Avenue in Fort Lauderdale. Early congregants included Moe Katz, a real estate salesman, and his brother, Mack. Both are believed to be buried in the B'nai Israel section of the Evergreen Cemetery on Southeast 10th Avenue in Fort Lauderdale.

Mother Nature was unkind to the new congregation. Shortly after they began services, the devastating hurricane of 1926 destroyed the building's second floor. The area was devastated.

But the young congregation persevered. It met in various buildings until they built their own in 1937. At South Andrews Avenue and 18th Street, the congregation held its first services for the High Holy Days during this year. It practiced in this location until members moved to nearby Lauderdale Lakes in 1968. In subsequent decades, the growing congregation helped spawn other congregations.

Early members recount impediments to a flourishing Jewish culture. Some recall hotel signage during the 1950s and 1960s with euphemisms like Restricted Clientele. Some neighborhoods had "restricted covenant" clauses written into property deeds, meaning that no Jews could move in. This was legal until the Civil Rights Act of 1964. "The older members say Fort Lauderdale's weather climate was warm, but the social climate was cold," said Rabbi Edward Maline.[9]

Congregation leaders encouraged interfaith efforts in part to counter discrimination. Ministerial associations held interfaith luncheons, for example.

Temple Emanu-El is credited for helping other congregations start. Beth El in Hollywood and Bat Yam in eastern Fort Lauderdale are two cited examples.

In 2001, Rabbi Maline noted that "because of its history and stability, Temple Emanu-El has come to represent Judaism to the larger community."[10] It was the spiritual home for Jewish pioneers.

In the 1980s and 1990s, the congregation attendance dropped. So did financial contributions. In 2004, the temple merged with Temple Kol Ami, which was founded in 1975.

Today, Temple Kol Ami is a thriving congregation on a sprawling campus. Yet its origins were humble. In the mid-1970s, just a handful of congregants met in different places within Plantation.

The merger was bittersweet for Temple Emanu-El. Rabbi Maline commented at the time, "What we're preserving is the name of the temple, the memorials, the ritual objects, so in that sense, Temple Emanu-El will be preserved. But we're also losing a little of our independence."[11]

At the time of merger in 2004, Temple Kol Ami had about 1,100 families and Temple Emanu-El about 200.

Arial and interior views of Temple Kol Ami, now merged with Temple Emanu-El, which began in 1926. The founding members rented a room above a restaurant on Andrews Avenue in Fort Lauderdale.

Ramat Shalom
11301 W Broward Boulevard
Phone: (954) 947-8083
Website: www.ramatshalom.org

Started in 1976, Ramat Shalom is one of the oldest synagogues in Broward County. Its origins are rather untraditional, dating to a discussion group meeting in various members' living rooms. As it grew, it became a congregation with a synagogue and rabbi. In its early decades, it was part of the Reconstructionist movement.

Linda and Garry Wachtel were among its early founders. Linda explained that part of her interest in Reconstructionist Judaism was equality for women. "We had daughters and wanted then to have an equal place in Judasim."[12] Early prayer books had translations so that members who did not read Hebrew could follow along. The synagogue also had another distinction—it was among the first in the area to use guitars in its services.

Today, Ramat Shalom is a cross of Reconstructionist and Reform and has about three hundred families.

Hollywood

Morse Arcade (Became Temple Sinai of Hollywood)

The first Jewish prayer services in Hollywood were held in this spot. A Tekila Bar Club, this is one of Hollywood's oldest commercial buildings.

The rear storefront was the meeting place of the Jewish Community Center of Hollywood in 1942. From this sprung forth the congregation of Temple Sinai of Hollywood, located on North 46th Avenue.

Temple Sinai of Hollywood (Present-Day Location)
1400 North 46th Avenue
Phone: (954) 987-0026
Website: www.sinaihollywood.com

Starting around the Morse Arcade on Hollywood Boulevard in 1942, Temple Sinai of Hollywood set up its permanent location in early 1943. The Conservative congregation thrived during the post-World War II period, though it has experienced some decline in subsequent decades. In 1994, it relocated to its current location on North 46th Avenue. Next to the main sanctuary is a full-service Judaica shop offering items like tableware, candle holders, and hostess gifts.

Try the e-services on the webpage, where you can listen to a selection of classical and contemporary tunes for an assortment of prayers.

Historic Cemeteries

Fort Lauderdale

Evergreen Cemetery, B'nai Israel Section
1300 SE 10th Avenue
Phone: (954) 745-2140
Website: www.lauderdalememorialpark.com

This is likely the oldest Jewish cemetery in Broward County. Established in the auspicious year of 1926, the year of the devastating hurricane, it marks the burial place for some of the City of Fort Lauderdale's earliest residents. Many buried here were members of the pioneering Temple Emanu-El. Today, that congregation is merged with Temple Kol Ami. (See page 153.)

Those buried in Evergreen Cemetery include Moe Katz, along with his brother, Mack, "known for Mack's Ladies' Shop, reputed to be the first women's clothing store in town, and his wife Sadye,

B'nai Israel section of Evergreen Cemetery is likely the oldest Jewish cemetery in Broward County, established in 1926. It is the burial place of some of Fort Lauderdale's earliest residents, like Moe Katz. (Photo by Cynthia Foster.)

who helped spearhead building campaigns for the local War Memorial Auditorium."[13] Members of the Sterling family of Sterling's Men and Boys Store also rest in the cemetery.

Tips for the Traveler: The cemetery is easily accessible and open to the public. It's not large, so you should find the corner that is walled off with the white archway bearing the words B'nai Israel (Children of Israel) in Hebrew lettering. The archway also has a Star of David and a small gate. The tombstones are marked with Hebrew lettering. Some have small rocks on them rather than flowers, per the Jewish custom.

Festivals

Jewish American Heritage Month

May in Florida marks Jewish American Heritage Month. It began in 2006 when Pres. George W. Bush issued the proclamation. The significance is to recognize Jewish Americans for their contributions to the United States.

Check local listings for events. Some of the more famous in the area are musical performances at Florida International University and other venues. These concerts salute the multitude of influential Jewish composers like Leonard Bernstein, Ira and George Gershwin, Irving Berlin, Stephen Sondheim, and many more.

Other Museums and Cultural Attractions

These sites are not explicitly Jewish per this book's theme. However, they are very important to the origins and development of Fort Lauderdale, and their owners likely interacted with early Jewish settlers.

Bonnet House Museum and Gardens
900 N Birch Road
Phone: (954) 563-5393
Website: www.bonnethouse.org
Hours: Tues.–Sun., 9 a.m. to 4 p.m.; closed Mon. and on holidays
Admission: Adults $20

Tucked away near the ocean is a low-profile historic house and estate: the Bonnet House. It was named after the bonnet lily that floats along the rivers running through the property.

In 1895, in the very early days of Broward County, Hugh Birch acquired the property. He gifted it to his daughter Helen and her husband, artist Frederic Bartlett, in 1919. The property was located in what was then a remote area with wildlife. The thirty-five acres sit on the oceanfront and were purchased for just one dollar an acre! Fred recounted that when he came home he often did not know what he would find on the property; there were unexpected encounters with wildlife.

After Helen's death in 1925, a dejected Bartlett married Evelyn Lilly of the Eli Lilly fortune. The couple used the property as a winter residence for decades until Fred Bartlett's death in 1953. Thereafter, Evelyn continued to use it as a winter home until her death in 1997. Some of the estate staff also lived on the property with their families.

Conscious of historic preservation and without heirs of her own, Evelyn deeded the property to the Florida Trust for Historic Preservation. That organization runs the current museum and gardens for the public.

Evelyn willed the estate to a public trust in order to safeguard its future. She felt strongly that the public should see the property similar to how it looked in its earlier days. She worried about overdevelopment in the once remote area.

If her goal was to raise public awareness about the property while preserving its authenticity, it would be realized in a way she could never have imagined. The property was featured as the finish line for a season of the critically acclaimed reality series *The Amazing Race.*

The estate in some ways harkens to a quiet, leisurely lifestyle enjoyed by those of means. Bonnet House director Robert Kauth said in 1995 after Evelyn made her final winter visit, "It's the end of an era, a time that reflected a slow and genteel period in the history of this country and certainly of Fort Lauderdale."[14]

The main residence, which is open for tours, was designed by Bartlett to take on the appearance of a Caribbean plantation house. The island's vibrant colors are mimicked in the house.

The gardens surrounding the house contain rare plants, trees, and wildlife the Bartletts kept from their global travels. The grounds have a larger significance. The estate contains one of the only remaining native barrier island habitats. It is a home for ecosystems: the beach, fresh water slough, mangrove wetlands, and a maritime forest. Contrasting with this lush ground is a desert garden also on the property.

Evelyn had two passions when it came to the outdoors: orchids and monkeys. She collected a variety of orchids, and the estate today celebrates orchid festivals. She also enjoyed interacting with the monkeys who lived on the land. Evelyn purchased dozens of monkeys when she first started developing the property. She is said to have offered them strawberry jam, one of their favorites. Monkeys still roam the estate. Evelyn's interest in monkeys is also shown in the monkey art in the living room.

Both Fred and Evelyn knew heartbreak. She was married to the grandson of Eli Lilly, but it ended in a tumultuous divorce. Fred, the son of a prominent hardware company, was widowed twice.

The two met in Beverly, Massachusetts, and continued to reside there during the warmer months. They were prominent art

The Bonnet House is named for bonnet lilies that float along the rivers running through the property. (Photo by Paul M. Kaplan.)

collectors; some of the paintings collected turned out to be very famous in later decades.

Bonnet House has a sense of humor to it, a lightness not present in other historic houses. A former director commented on the house's décor: "The whole thing is tongue-in-cheek, displaying a sophisticated and subtle humor that pervaded the lives of its owners."[15]

Sadly, there are threats to the house's future with non-stop massive development nearby. Accordingly, the National Trust for Historic Preservation included the Bonnet House in its Save America's Treasures program.

Mother Nature has also been unkind to it. Hurricanes Katrina and Wilma greatly hurt much of the estate's upper tree canopy.

Tips for the Traveler: Start with the tour of the property and house. On the tour, you'll watch a video with Evelyn Bartlett and will learn more about the house and why she willed it to a public trust. Then you can browse some of the art she and Fred painted.

The estate was a place of leisure. As one former director put it, "It is a fashionable quirky. A place of a lot of laughter, love and carefree living happened."[16] So enjoy the colorful tiles, carousel animals scattered about the outdoor hallways, and courtyards.

In addition to the house tour, I recommend a naturist tour of the outside trails. Check in at the gift shop, and a naturist will take you out. You can also explore the extensive trails on your own. You'll see a variety of flora and fauna and could meet some monkeys along the way!

The monthly orchid greenhouse tour, conducted by a curator who specializes in the flowers, is perfect for orchid lovers. About 1,500 are in the collection. Reserve your spot on this tour before your visit.

Because the daily house tour does not show the second floor (private living quarters), there is a behind-the-scenes private living quarters tour. My recommendation is that you start with the house and nature tour. If you are very interested in the property and learning more about the lives and interests the Bartletts, sign up for this. It occurs monthly, so scheduling may be inconvenient. Yet it has several advantages over the regular tours. First, groups are smaller (usually ten or fewer) so you will be able to ask more questions. Second, the docents leading this tour are usually more experienced. Think of it as the advanced class. Tours are also offered in Spanish.

I also recommend the Orchid Festival if you are around in the beginning of December and if you have a passion for orchids. There are lectures, green markets, and sometimes complimentary refreshments. You can also purchase orchids that are normally difficult to find. If you're not available in December but are interested in this topic, sign up for the monthly orchid greenhouse tour.

Another idea is to attend the Young Artist Music Series. You'll hear selections from local college students. It's a great way to support tomorrow's musicians.

Fort Lauderdale Historic Society
219 SW 2nd Avenue
Phone: (954) 463-4431
Website: www.fortlauderdalehistoricalsociety.org
Hours: Mon.-Fri., 12:00 p.m.,-4:00 p.m.; Sat. and Sun., 9:30 a.m.-4:00 p.m.
Admission: Adults $15

Learn more about the City of Fort Lauderdale's history at the Fort Lauderdale Historic Society. There are a several historic buildings located next to each other: a 1907 house museum and three other 1905 houses. This campus also includes a comprehensive research facility with a photo collection.

Exhibitions are on various topics but tend to focus on the theme of how macro events have affected a local community. For example, it poses the question of how World War impacted Fort Lauderdale. It occasionally has exhibits on Jewish themes.

The museum also profiles a little-known subject: What was the land like before the 1800s? Some exhibits mention the prehistoric Glades Culture and the Tequesta who roamed the land and rivers. It notes that by 1763, few remained. Then in the 1820s the Seminole Indians appeared in Broward County along with Caucasian planters.

The city's name derives from a military major, William Lauderdale. He led a team to overtake Seminole lands. For subsequent decades, it was sparsely populated land until Frank Stranahan settled there and developed it in 1893. In 1896, the Florida East Coast Railway transformed the region.

Tips for the Traveler: Start by visiting the museum at the New River Inn. It operated as a twenty-four guest room hotel until 1955.

I recommend the tour of historic houses, since most of the buildings other than the museum are not open for self-guiding. The other buildings include:

- Edwin King House, which was used as a boarding house for soldiers' wives during World War II.
- The Acetylene Building, erected in 1905, that housed an acetylene gas generator to provide light to nearby houses.
- The King-Cromartie House, built in 1907, was originally in Smoker Park. In 1971, it was transported by barge to this location. It weighed a mere 150 tons.
- The Hoch Heritage Library and Research Center was originally a post office annex. Today, it houses the society's historic collections. It is open to the public for research. Also look for any photos you would like to purchase.

Keep an eye out for a replica of what a small schoolhouse would have looked like in 1899. Ivy Cromartie, wife of Frank Stranahan, was the first teacher in Broward County and played a very important role in its development. She also advanced many causes for Seminole Indians.

There are walking tours of old neighborhoods in the city as well as haunted ghost tours. Inquire at the museum.

Stranahan House
335 SE 6th Avenue
Phone: (954) 524-4736
Website: www.stranahanhouse.org
Hours: Guided tours are provided daily (Mon.–Sun.) at 1, 2, and
3 p.m.
Admission: Adults $12.00

The Stranahan House is the oldest surviving structure in Broward
County. The history of Fort Lauderdale is embodied within its
walls.

The historic house located on the famed Los Olas Boulevard in
downtown Fort Lauderdale was built in 1901 by Frank Stranahan
when Broward County was in its infancy. The father of Fort
Lauderdale, he moved to the New River Settlement, as the area
was called, and played a central role in its development.

The prominent Seminole Indians were key in Stranahan's life,
the house, and the area. At a time when relations between settlers
and the Seminole were very strained, Stranahan built strong
relationships with them. He gained the reputation for being fair.
He traded with them.

The building was first a trading post, then a community center,
later a post office, and finally a home to the Stranahans in 1906.
The town was just springing to life. The 1910 census counts 142
residents in the town. No one could have imagined that in decades
this area would be a spring break hub for college party-goers.

Meanwhile, the growing community needed a teacher. Ivy
Cromartie took the job. She was particularly engaged with the
Seminole children and offered informal lessons at the trading posts.
She differed from many other teachers in that she did not try to
change the tribe's traditions. Some Seminoles spoke of how Ivy
and Frank gave them their first pair of shoes so they could walk to
school. Ivy gained the trust of the tribe's leaders. She built an
enduring and deep friendship with the Seminole people.

Frank was the town's first banker, postmaster, and businessman,
and Ivy was the first school teacher. The museum tells the story
that Ivy agreed to marry Frank only if he agreed not to have
children and to shave his beard.

The Stranahans played a central role in the budding city. Ivy was focused on women's rights and suffrage as well as teaching the Seminole Indian children. Museum literature says that "throughout her life Ivy would be involved with virtually every civic and social cause in the city."[17]

Her relationship with the Seminoles was tested when in 1924 the federal government asked her to convince the tribe to relocate to the reservation. It was a controversial move. She honored the government's request and gave assurances to the tribe that the relocation would be in their interest. Trusting her words, they agreed.

The Stranahan House is the oldest surviving structure in Broward County. (Photo by Paul M. Kaplan.)

The couple's fortune followed that of the area. In the 1920s, his banking business thrived with the large amount of borrowing and building going on at the time. But in 1926, the market crashed. That same year, the Great Hurricane of 1926 devastated the area. Another hurricane followed in two years' time. Frank's business was in tatters. Many of his loans could not be paid back.

Frank was impacted greatly. In 1929, he wrote in his diary, "My wife gave me much encouragement, but I can't seem to grasp it."[18]

Sadly, he committed suicide in the late 1920s. It was a huge blow to Ivy. In grief, she wore black for more than ten years. As a widow, Ivy then lived in the house for several decades, leasing out the first floor for extra money and turning part of it into a restaurant. She returned to her social and civic causes, about which she was so passionate for many decades. She fought for a hospital for local African Americans. Continuing with her work with the Seminole Indians, she championed for their education, healthcare, and land.

After Ivy's death in 1971, the house was recognized for its historical value. She bequeathed it to her church, the Seventh Day Adventist Church. The Fort Lauderdale Historical Society purchased it in 1975. It was then restored in the 1980s to its initial appearance and was operated as a historic house museum.

A curator summarized its quiet eloquence. "The house is unique in that it's simple, but in its simplicity, it is beautiful."[19]

Tips for the Traveler: Take a tour offered daily of the house museum. The caretaker—who has worked there for almost three decades—may be available to answer additional questions. Sometimes, he is at the gift shop.

There's also a ghost tour that includes a visit inside the house. You'll learn about tales of the supernatural. Part of the tour is on the river in a water taxi.

Halloween and Christmas are seasonal times to visit. For Halloween, there are sometimes special ghost tours. For Christmas, you can see the house's splendor as it is decorated in a Victorian Christmas theme.

Notable Eateries

Fort Lauderdale

Fort Lauderdale is home to several Jewish-style delis. The three here are open only for breakfast and lunch and usually close in the mid-afternoon. Offerings are similar from one to another: egg creams (cream, seltzer, and syrup); overstuffed deli sandwiches with assortments of corned beef, pastrami, and smoked fish on a usually beautifully decorated platter; salads; kosher hotdogs; potato pancakes; wraps; and much more.

Still, each has a unique theme:

- NY Deli, as its name suggests, is about New York nostalgia. It proclaims, "Here we don't just talk the talk, we serve it up to you with coleslaw."[20] Classic New York photos adorn the walls and website.
- Top Hat Deli takes its name from owner Elliot's grandfather, Max Wolf, who left Germany for New York City in 1936. Of all his possessions, what he brought with him in this urgent move was his top hat. The hat was passed down several generations. Times and fashions changed, but the importance of the top hat for the family

Top Hat Deli, one of Fort Lauderdale's New York-style delis. (Photo by Cynthia Foster.)

remained. Now a fourth-generation family member wears the top hat in photos that adorn the deli.

• Pomperdale Deli dates back to 1969. It also has New York nostalgia. Pomperdale counts itself as the sixth New York borough. The website acknowledges: "In New York City, every neighborhood has its deli. One would never have to travel far to find an awesome pastrami on rye, homemade turkey, corned beef, or lox. But for most native New Yorkers, things took a big change on the migration south. What was once a five-minute walk, has become a 20-minute drive in the quest to find a taste of the homeland—and yes, we still do mean New York."[21] Recently, Larry Bruskin, a "self-described deli guy," revamped the deli and introduced new recipes.

Café Emunah
3558 N Ocean Boulevard
Phone: (954) 561-6411
Website: http://www.myemunah.com

This kosher seafood restaurant offers fresh sushi and fish. It was cofounded by Chabad Rabbi Moishe M. Lipszyc. His aim was to offer "an experience for the senses and an oasis for the mind, body and soul as a physical journey into one's spiritual self."[22] The restaurant's name, Emunah, means "faith." The café is part of the Galt Ocean Mile area on the same block as a mikvah for men and women, a pre-school with a playground, a Hebrew school, a Sunday school, and a Lubavitch synagogue.

Ask about events usually in the winter on Kabbalah (Jewish mysticism) or other topics, as well as personal growth seminars on health-related topics.

The website contains advice and essays. One, for example, is about the true meaning of humility.

Grand Café
2905 Stirling Road
Phone: (954) 986-6860
Website: www.grandcafe.us

This Middle Eastern-oriented eatery was opened in early 2012 by two childhood friends from Israel. Their lives have been intertwined over many years through sports, military service, and now the restaurant business.

Besides signature drinks, Grand Café offers a plethora of Israeli specialty items like beet carpaccio (beets with goat cheese and vinegar on a baguette), caprese (mozzarella cheese, sliced tomatoes, and pesto sauce), spicy tuna taco, and a Greek plate, among many other selections.

Hoffman Chocolates
920 E Las Olas Boulevard
Phone: (954) 368-4320
Website: http://www.hoffmans.com

Walking down Las Olas Boulevard, you'll come across one of the Hoffman Chocolate stores. The kosher chocolate shop started in Lake Worth, Florida, about forty miles north of Fort Lauderdale. Paul Hoffman, the former engineer turned entrepreneur, bought the shop. His journey took him from aircrafts to chocolate; he left Pratt and Whitney Aircraft Company to found the store.

Hoffman had to learn the business and how to make great chocolate. So he attended candy school in Erie, Pennsylvania. In his chocolatier infancy, he made creams and marshmallows. Then he offered more chocolate products and started a factory in West Palm Beach.

By 1987, he purchased land in Greenacres, not far from West Palm Beach. Today, that space houses the factory, retail store, and corporate offices.

Since then, it is has expanded to about ten stores mostly in South Florida. They offer the usual assortment of milk and dark chocolates, truffles, and chocolate fruits. They also have seasonal gifts like the Hanukah gift basket, Hanukah gelt, and chocolate dreidels.

In Greenacres, you can visit the chocolate factory and watch the chocolate-making process through observation windows. As is the case in most chocolate factories, their production facility is divided into three lines for milk, dark, and white chocolate. A separate molding area is dedicated to making two- and three-dimensional chocolates. There is also an ice cream shop and gardens.

The candies and chocolates are all kosher, which comes with unexpected benefits. For example, "the marshmallow formulation was changed to use kosher fish gelatin instead of animal gelatin, resulting in enhancement in both flavor and texture."[23]

It's a multi-generational business with Hoffman's daughter playing an executive role in the company.

There are also chocolate-making classes at the factory. Call to inquire and to make reservations.

Sunrise

Milky Café
4597 N Pine Island Road
Phone: (954) 533-5325
Website: www.milkycafe.com

This strictly kosher café offers vegetarian and dairy-free options. Try the combination plate of kebeh, mozzarella sticks, spring rolls, and potato pastel.

Sunrise Pita
2680 N University Drive
Phone: (954) 748-0090

This Sunrise-based informal Israeli food establishment is a cheap, fast option. The food is standard Middle Eastern with falafel, shawarma, kebabs with various sauces, hummus, grape leaves, and chili sauces, among many other items.

Hollywood

Levy's Kosher of Hollywood
3369 Sheridan Street
Phone: (954) 983-2825
Website: www.levyskosherofhollywood.com

This family-owned, Middle Eastern, informal restaurant serves many familiar items like shawarma and kebabs.

Chapter Five

Palm Beach County

Jewish settlement of the county began largely in West Palm Beach in the mid-1890s with the advent of Henry Flagler's railway. No longer was the region isolated from other parts of the state. A few families congregated around Clematis Street downtown, including Isidor Cohen and Jake Schnieidman. They formed Temple Beth Israel in West Palm Beach in 1923. Temple Beth El followed a few years later. The early 1920s saw rapid building and expansion, only to be dramatically arrested by the Great Hurricane in 1926. The Jewish population of the county in the 1930s was less than that of Broward or Miami. As late as 1940, the Jewish population of Palm Beach County hovered at one thousand. Harry and Florence Brown of St. Louis were the first Jews to settle in Boca Raton, in 1931. After World War II, though, residents in search of more space were moving north. Suburbs became popular. In addition, during this time, more snowbirds began visiting the area and staying for the winter. Some purchased second homes. Still, the Jewish population was small in the county during this period.

By the 1970s, Jewish community centers and Jewish federations were founded in Boca Raton. Thousands of retirees from northeastern states took advantage of deals from developers like H. Irwin Levy, who built Century Village, a predominantly Jewish development in suburban West Palm Beach. By 1980, the Jewish population had grown to one hundred thousand. In the 1980s, 1990s, and 2000s, Jews increasingly moved north from Miami-Dade and Broward County into Palm Beach County. Consequently, Palm Beach County has one of the largest Jewish population densities in the state. It is estimated that about 20 percent of the overall county population is Jewish. In some areas, like Boca Raton, it is almost half. Today, there are about fifty synagogues in Palm Beach County and a thriving Chabad movement.

There are many exiting venues to explore. Find out how Henry Flagler's railroad transformed the once remote region at the Henry Flagler Museum. Visit the hidden gem of the Jewish Sound Archives at Florida Atlantic University Library. Catch a performance of the Klezmer Company Orchestra, the only academic-library-affiliated Klezmer group of its kind. View an engaging film and participate in lively discussion at Café Cinematheque. Trace the histories of the county's many synagogues at the little-known Nathan D. Rosen Museum at the Levis Jewish Community Center.

Museums

Boca Raton

The Boca Raton Museum of Art
501 Plaza Real
Phone: (561) 392-2500
Website: https://www.bocamuseum.org
Hours: Tues., Wed., and Fri., 10 a.m.–5 p.m.; Thurs., 10 a.m.–8 p.m.; Sat. and Sun., 12 p.m.–5 p.m.; closed Mon.
Admission: $12 Adults

The museum has permanent collections in nineteenth and twentieth century European and American paintings, modern masters (which are mostly early twentieth century artists like Modigliani), abstract sculpture from the 1970s and 1980, and the art of West Africa.

As far as Jewish subjects, the museum has pieces from Amedeo Modigliani, Roy Lichtenstein, Helen Frankenthaler, and others.

Temporary exhibits often reflect on Jewish themes. In 2016, *Memories of the Shtetl* showcased "memory paintings" of artist Samuel Rothbort's small native Czarist village. He depicts daily life in mostly Jewish villages, or shtetls. Nostalgic and colorful, some present a brighter depiction than what is commonly thought of with shtetls. His paintings inspired a 1961 documentary by Harriet Semegram called *Memories of the Shtetl* and the 1964 hit musical *Fiddler on the Roof*.

West Palm Beach

Norton Museum of Art in West Palm Beach
1451 S Olive Avenue
Phone: (561) 832-5196
Website: www.norton.org
Hours: Tues.–Sun., 12 p.m.–5 p.m. (Thurs. open until 9 p.m.)
Admission: Free for all visitors until December 2018

The Norton Museum of Art dates back to 1941. Its permanent exhibit includes American art, Chinese art, Contemporary art, European art, and photography. It exhibits paintings from Jewish artists like David Levinthal, Robert Rauschenberg, and Marc Chagall.

The Norton Museum is known for its film series, which at times corresponds with exhibits. For instance, *Many Faces of Israel* and *This Place: Israel Through Photography's Lens* were presented in conjunction with a series of short films on the diversity of Israel shot through the lens of black Bedouin students and Jewish Orthodox students. The series aims to showcase the "human side of Israel, too often overlooked in the political debate."[1]

Cinema Screenings and Performing Arts
Palm Beach
Café Cinematheque International
Phone: (561) 347-8509
Facebook: www.facebook.com/Cafe-Cinematheque-International

In 2000, film scholar and enthusiast Shelly Isaacs founded Café Cinematheque, a program of award-winning and internationally acclaimed foreign language films that is held in theaters, universities, libraries, and cultural arts venues throughout South Florida. Isaacs loves regaling an audience with insights into the process of filmmaking, as well as contextual and cultural implications, backstories, and references of each film.

As host and commentator, Isaacs introduces the film, screens it, and then stirs a compelling and entertaining discussion afterwards. He has been the host of the annual International Film Series for the Boca Museum of Art since 2004, teaches film appreciation at Florida International University and Florida Atlantic University, and has been a judge for the Fort Lauderdale International Film Festival. He offers film programs for the Broward County Library System and at the Aventura Performing Arts and Cultural Center. Since 2009, Isaacs has also brought his passion and expertise to sea with his Cinematheque at Sea program, which takes passengers on film cruises to the Cannes International Film Festival and throughout the Caribbean.

If you reside in the Palm Beach area and appreciate international film, consider one of his classes. You can also ask Isaacs about his advertising past. As well as being a creative director, writer, and

Shelly Isaacs, founder of Café Cinematheque, a program of varied film screenings and discussions held throughout arts venues in South Florida.

producer at some of America's top agencies, he worked on many film campaigns, among them notable and groundbreaking films such as *Kramer vs. Kramer* with Dustin Hoffman in 1979, *Superman* in 1978, and the classic comedy *Arthur*. Some of his film series are Jewish themed. For example, in 2000 he created the Boca Raton Film Forum on the Jewish-American experience conveyed on film.

Obtaining original prints from Brandeis University archives, he screened nine classic films in association with Temple Beth-El of Boca Raton, the Florida Atlantic University Business of Film program, and the Fort Lauderdale International Film Festival. These events featured guest speakers, among them the Academy Award-winning director Arthur Hiller (*The Man in the Glass Booth*) and a member of the prosecuting team at the Nuremburg trials in Germany (*Judgment at Nuremburg*). Other programs have included *The Last Mensch, Phoenix from Germany, Live and Become,* and *To*

Life. He especially seeks out Jewish-themed films from cultures throughout the world, hoping to challenge his audiences and facilitate discussions on "the Diaspora, dislocation, identity, isolation, heritage, traditions, the Holocaust and much more."[2]

West Palm Beach

Raymond Kravis Center for the Performing Arts
701 Okeechobee Boulevard
Phone: (561) 832-7469
Website: www.kravis.org

For over sixty years, this downtown site was Connie Mack Field, named after the famous baseball player. At the highest point in West Palm Beach, it was the spring training camp for the Philadelphia Athletics and St. Louis Browns. Legendary baseball players like Babe Ruth, Lou Gehrig, and Jackie Robinson were among those who practiced here.

In September 1992, the performing arts center turned a new page in its expansion. The grand opening was a glittering week of free performances by famed Carnegie Hall violinist Isaac Stern and comedian Lillian Tomlin. By 1995, there were three venues: a concert hall, playhouse, and amphitheater. The Miami City Ballet, Palm Beach Opera, and Palm Beach Pops perform here. A staggering 550 performances take place each season. The center also offers reduced or free tickets to thousands of economically disadvantaged senior citizens and community groups.

Some notable Jewish comedians and actors such as Woody Allen and Mandy Patinkin have performed here as well.

The center was named after Raymond Kravis, a noted Jewish oil and gas consultant and philanthropist from Tulsa, Oklahoma. He and his wife wintered in West Palm Beach for over thirty years. He was an active supporter of the arts and also was associated with Pres. John F Kennedy's father, Joseph P. Kennedy. Kravis found oil deals for the elder Kennedy.

Kravis was quite active in Jewish causes. He was elected to the National Campaign Cabinet of the US Jewish Appeal, a prominent humanitarian organization, and held key positions within several other Jewish philanthropic groups.

The Donald M. Ephraim Palm Beach Jewish Film Festival
Locations vary, check website
Phone: (877) 318-0071
Website: www.pbjff.org

Check out the Jewish film festival in late January. Founded in 1990, the festival has expanded in scope and audience in recent years and shows at several venues across the country. If you make films on Jewish subjects, consider submitting. Instructions are on the website.

Festival director Ellen Wedner explains the festival's development: "Twenty some years ago, when Jewish film festivals were just beginning, distributors did not see the potential in marketing through us. Over the years, we've created a very powerful, vocal audience all over the United States and Canada."[3]

The festival runs about three weeks, usually at four or five venues. In addition to feature-length films, the festival also screens documentaries and shorts. Organizers emphasize its universality. Wedner notes, "These films are not religious. In many cases, they are about culture, tradition, history, art, spirituality, interaction with other groups. So if you have an interest in the world, something is going to draw you in."[4]

Special Library Collections

Boca Raton

Judaica Sound Archives and Klezmer Company Orchestra at Florida Atlantic University
777 Glades Road
Phone: (561) 297-0080
Website: rsa.fau.edu

Tucked away on the Florida Atlantic University is a gem few locals know about. The collection of Jewish music, printed albums, cantorial music, and Klezmer music is unparalleled for any university library.

Recorded Sound Archive (RSA)
The Recorded Sound Archive (RSA) located on the Boca Raton campus is a digital library of vintage Jewish and other music.

Established in 2002, the initiative was to preserve Jewish music. Since then, it has blossomed into digitizing music for all types of sound recordings and is open to the public.

In 2009, the collection expanded to Jazz and early American vintage recordings. But visiting this archive is more than just taking a trip to a music library. It's a journey to the past. It's hearing vintage recordings as they originally sounded. The museum has "vintage players like the Edison cylinder player from 1913, a 1918 wind up phonograph, a 1924 electric Victrola and a 1960s tape deck. Some say it is like 'taking a walk through the early years of sound recording.'"[5]

You can search for and listen to music on the website unless there are copyright restrictions, in which case you can hear snippets. Follow the instructions to register.

The music varies from the humorous ("How Much Is That Pickle in the Window") to the retrospective (*100+ Years of Zionism–A Musical Journey*) to the folksy (*1960 Newport Folk Festival* and *20th Century Yiddish Humor*). Other albums are of children's songs. Besides Judaica music, collections include vintage children's music and jazz.

Beyond promoting sound is the museum's focus on the artistry of records. Today, music is usually listened to on streaming sites. But, for some, the music loses something that way. Album cover aesthetics have also been recovered in the collection, which features one hundred rare picture book records with original artwork from the 1940s.

RSA provides music digitization; scholarly research on genres; sound restoration; preservation; and rescue of records and CDs that may otherwise be discarded.

I recommend you spend time listening to the abundance of digitized music. You can access it on your smartphone, tablet, or desktop. If possible, visit the video library for a unique experience. Appointments are required.

If you are local and looking to volunteer, RSA is looking for help in its operations. It also seeks donations of old music.

Jewish Print Music Collection

Another initiative is the Jewish Print Music Collection dating from 1897 to the present. Think about the scores, manuscripts, notes, etc. that go into producing music. This collection puts it together. "It also houses a very large collection of American Yiddish theater music, comprised [sic] of piano-vocal scores spanning the years of 1890-1960."[6]

The collection is more than an aggregate of printed materials. It's a window into the culture, language, and literature of the Jewish Diaspora. When sheet music was at its prime in the late nineteenth and early twentieth centuries, sheet covers were often colorful and artistic. Many are in this collection. These covers shed light on "visual folk art from the period and offer additional cultural insight through imagery."[7]

The collection categories are American popular, classical, Jewish, and cantorial. The repertories vary, too, among solos, instrumental only, chamber ensembles, and several other varieties.

A sub-section specializes in archives of notable cantors and rabbis. Importantly, the collection is more than just scores and choral music—it provides the personal papers that give insights into the rabbi's or cantor's imagination.

You can visit the facility through an appointment for individuals or groups by calling (561) 297-0080. You can also ask about volunteer opportunities.

Klezmer Company Orchestra and Shelf to Stage Program

Aaron Kula serves as the director for music performance and education at Florida Atlantic University and holds a faculty appointment in the library. In this role, he created unique programs like Shelf to Stage and the Klezmer Company Orchestra (KCO) in the late 1990s.

The KCO performs music in a unique setting. It's a professional ensemble-in-residence at FAU Libraries, the only ensemble at an academic library in the United States.

KCO has toured and performed at various music festivals. It also has concerts open to the public, although some events are private. Check the website (www.klezmercompany.com/concerts) for the latest. Kula says, "If someone comes to our concert, he or she will experience anything and everything."[8] The NuKlezmerClassix concert is an anticipated event for the annual Kultur Festival in March. Held over eight days, the festival showcases new Klezmer music and provides lectures on its historical and sociological context. It also shows films and hosts comedians. Examples of program titles

Aaron Kula performing with a Klezmer music orchestra with historical music reimagined through new arrangements. Some revised compositions have a Latin, Caribbean, or Cuban beat. (Courtesy KCO and FAU Libraries.)

at the festivals are Moroccan Soul with the Klezmer Company Trio and Jewish Melodies in Jazztime. The festival is open to the public. Visit fauevents.com for information on the current season.

You can also purchase CDs if interested. One is *Klezmerology*, which has ten Latin Klezmer songs like "2nd Avenue Mambo" and "Bongos and Bulgars." Some can be downloaded on iTunes or streamed. See more at www.klezmercompany.com/discography.php.

For the Shelf to Stage program, Aaron and his staff choose historical music buried in the collection and compile new arrangements, orchestrations, and compositions. It breathes life into old music. The goal is to not let the scores remain shelved but to have them played by today's musicians. Kula re-imagines a score note by note, transitioning it from a late nineteenth century piece to make it suitable for today's orchestra. Often, he adds a Cuban, Caribbean, or Latin beat. Kula notes that this provides a local flavor, given the culture of South Florida. The piece is thus recalibrated musically and given new life through performances. This effort also rescues the physical sheet music. Most of these scores were printed to be played in residential living rooms. Through this effort, the new scores have a fresh format.[9]

You can view the full scores online and listen to performances by the KCO. Choose between folk, Klezmer, cantorial, and popular.

Genealogical Societies
Delray Beach

Jewish Genealogical Society of Palm Beach County
9085 Hagen Ranch Road
Phone: (561) 450-9577
Website: www.jgspalmbeachcounty.org

The organization was founded in 1990 by three members around a kitchen table. Today, it offers an extensive research library with five research collections pertaining to community and genealogy. It also gives monthly lectures, conferences, assistance with genealogical research techniques, and a mentoring program. If interested, sign up for their quarterly newsletter, Scattered Seeds.

Notable Hotels
Palm Beach

The Breakers Palm Beach
1 S County Road
Phone: (888) 727-1649
Website: www.thebreakers.com

One of the most famous hotels in the world, the Breakers is worth a visit, or at least a look, even if you are not staying there. In its early days, the Breakers discriminated against Jews and other groups. Today, though, many Jewish organizations hold conventions there, including Hadassah and the Anti-Defamation League.

The Breakers was built by Henry Flagler, one of the most prominent developers in the region. It's not a stretch to say his efforts changed Palm Beach forever. By expanding the railroad into the region, he opened up the once remote area.

Perhaps lesser known about Flagler was his hotel building. In 1894, he built his first in this area: the Royal Poinciana Hotel at Lake Worth. Two years later, he built the Palm Beach Inn. Guests asked for rooms "over by the breakers." With this in mind, Flagler renamed it the Breakers.

On June 9, 1903, the Breakers burned down, but it was rebuilt fairly quickly. Rooms were offered at $4 per night, which included three meals a day. Using a common inflation calculator, that would be $113 in 2017. Still a great bargain!

The industrialists—or robber barons, to some—seemed to enjoy visiting. Guests included the Astors, Carnegies, Vanderbilts, and Rockefellers.

Flagler died in 1913. He only lived to see the hotel for a few years.

The mid-1920s were not kind to the hotel. Another fierce fire walloped the all-wood building. The subsequent hurricane of 1926 complicated matters. His heirs restored the Breakers, modeling it after the Villa Medici in Rome. To create a building with Italian authenticity, the hotel hired seventy-five artisans from Italy to finish the ceiling and lobby paintings.

Boca Resort and Club
501 East Camino Real
Phone: (888) 543-1277
Website: www.bocaresort.com

This famous resort was originally the Cloister Inn, built in 1926. The resort then was exclusive and restrictive. Many groups, including Jews, were not permitted to attend. In the 1940s, the resort changed hands. The once penniless Latvian-Jewish immigrant turned hotel magnate Myer Schine purchased the property in 1946. Under his ownership, the resort expanded its function. It also became a place to house art exhibits.

Today, it is a Waldorf Astoria Resort.

Community Organizations
Greater Palm Beach Area

Jewish Community Center of Greater Palm Beach
5221 Hood Road
Phone: (561) 712-5200
Website: www.jcconline.com

On this campus are two institutions: the Harold and Sylvia Kaplan JCC of Greater Palm Beach and the Jewish Federation of Palm Beach County. The JCC offers a variety of programming for all ages, including monthly Shabbat dinners for seniors, a parenting center, and a fitness center. It also has a kosher bistro and bakery on site. At the gym, quotations from the Talmud are featured at each exercise machine. "Fortify yourself, build up your strength," reads one. You can work out and learn Talmud simultaneously.

As you walk into the lobby, you will notice a glass tower containing many pennies. The vision is to have six columns filled with one million pennies each. That, of course, translates to $60,000. The idea is to donate this amount to Yad Vashem, the Holocaust museum in Jerusalem

Nathan D. Rosen Museum Gallery at the Levis Jewish Community Center
9801 Donna Klein Boulevard
Phone: (561) 852-3200
Website: http://levisjcc.org/culture/art

An excellent collection of Judaica in Palm Beach is displayed at the Nathan D. Rosen Museum Gallery at the Levis JCC. The museum showcases exhibits of beaded wearable art, Judaica paper cuts, and creation jewelry. Other art depicts heroic deeds. For example, a New York artist exhibited tapestries depicting heroic women who risked their lives to save others during World War II.

The museum also offers the Biennial Juried Art Competition, which prizes $1,000 for the best in show. Art talks are often held with local art docents, art historians, artists, and academics.

Make art yourself in a class. Courses are in watercolor, silk scarf painting, beaded jewelry making, and digital photography.

Historic Synagogues

Boca Raton

Temple Beth El of Boca Raton
333 SW 4th Avenue
Phone: (561) 391-8900
Website: www.tbeboca.org

The first Jewish congregation in the Boca Raton area, Temple Beth El of Boca Raton was founded by a Catholic nun. Mother de la Croix, president of Marymount College, invited founding members to her campus. They began to worship there. Later, the nascent congregation moved to a Moravian church at Palmetto Park Road and 12th Avenue. In the 1970s, it relocated to 333 Southwest 4th Avenue.

It is one of the most prominent Reform congregations in the United States today.

Palm Beach

Palm Beach Synagogue
120 North County Road
Phone: (561) 838-9002
Website: www.palmbeachsynagogue.org

Located near the famed Breakers as well as the Bradley House, the Palm Beach Synagogue's charming exterior looks older than it really is. Some of the congregation was at nearby Temple Emanu-El in Palm Beach. In 1994, Rabbi Moshe and Dinie Scheiner formed a sub-community within Temple Emanu-El that eventually became the modern Orthodox Palm Beach Synagogue.

The exterior of Palm Beach Synagogue is made to look older than the building really is. It houses a modern Orthodox congregation. (Photo by Aaron Davidson.)

Temple Beth El of Palm Beach
2815 N Flagler Drive
Phone: (561) 833-0339
Website: www.bethelwpb.com

Starting in the 1920s, a small number of Jews in West Palm Beach met in various members' homes. This was a common practice for many incipient Jewish communities. By 1924, the nascent congregation built Temple Beth Israel at 2020 Broward Avenue. This was the first Conservative synagogue in Palm Beach County. As Palm Beach's population increased, so did the congregation's membership. This accelerated during World War II.

By 1951, the congregation changed locations for more space. It moved into 1901 North Flagler Drive, where Temple Israel stands today.

Temple Beth Israel divided into the current Temple Israel and Temple Beth El. Temple Beth El found a home at 2815 N Flagler Drive.

Then the past became the present. The former building at 2020 Broward Avenue that housed the original Temple Beth Israel took on new functions. This time, it was the area's first Greek Orthodox Church and its associated American Hellenic Progressive Education. Later, the building changed hands again but continued as a house of worship. It became the Unitarian Society of Palm Beach. In keeping with its past of community service, it was utilized as a homeless shelter.

In 2006, its future became uncertain. A developer purchased the land to erect residential buildings. But the plans were not concrete.

The former building at 2020 Broward Avenue was in jeopardy of being knocked down. Congregation Beth El decided to buy the historic building at 2020 Broward Avenue from the developer WCI. In fact, according to some reports, WCI donated the building and contributed funds for it to be transported to its new location on 2815 N Flagler Drive near Temple Beth El. There are pictures of the building being transported on the highway.

Congregants then renovated the old 1,200 square foot chapel in its new location. The temple provided a new roof and drywall. The chapel was then used for morning services, educational programming, and special events. Temple Beth El had preserved the historic building and found new uses for it.

The temple's interior bears unique features. "Beth El's laminated acacia ceiling is in the shape of an ascending spiral that simulates the folds of a tent and culminates in a great window that floods the bima with light. The pews, which seat 900, are upholstered in bright orange and all face the bima at a 45-degree angle."[10]

In 2013, the fledgling Temple Beth Zion in Royal Palm Beach merged with Temple Beth El in West Palm Beach. The former's congregation was elderly and, for the most part, their descendants did not continue active membership.

Temple Emanu-El of Palm Beach
190 N County Road
Phone: (561) 832-0804
Website: www.tepb.org

In the early 1960s, a small group decided to establish a synagogue in Palm Beach. The group was meeting in a variety of venues: the Episcopal Church of Bethesda-by-the-Sea for Shabbat, at the Stouffer's Town House restaurant for Passover Seder, and at the Royal Poinciana Playhouse.

The congregation was looking for its first home. Finding it became an interfaith effort. Benjamin Lehr and local Christian clergy made it a reality. In 1964, Temple Emanu-El of Palm Beach's forty-five members met at its first location. It was in a storefront at 266 Sunrise Avenue.

By the early 1970s, the growing congregation outgrew its space. After a successful fundraising campaign, they relocated to its present site at 190 N County Road. By 1974, it opened the doors at its new venue. In the mid-1990s, it expanded the synagogue and added a new sanctuary.

Four elegant Mediterranean arches grace the stone building. Two curving stairways provide interesting angles. Inside, the sanctuary showcases arched stained glass windows and an ark door.

The temple maintains a high-quality gift shop. Shop for housewares, tableware, children's books, clothing, and jewelry items. It is open by appointment; contact the temple office. It is run by the Women's League of Temple Emanu-El of Palm Beach.

Belle Glade

Former Site of Temple Beth Sholom

In 1954, twenty-three local Jewish families built this one-room synagogue. It's significant as it was one of the first temples in a small-town in this region. Temple Emanu-El tells the often-overlooked story of small-town Jews. The congregation served as a "focal point for a small, tightly knit community of Jewish families."[11] Members were farmers, traders, produce distributors, dry-goods shop owners, and accountants. One family ran movie theaters.

At its zenith, the Glades Jewish community was about thirty-five families. The small synagogue had a part-time rabbi and a religious education program. Former members recount social events like charity balls. Others tell of joining together for an evening of raccoon hunting. Some enjoyed fishing.

The temple was led by a mail carrier in West Palm Beach, Jack Stateman. He was educated as a cantor and then was recruited as the temple's lay rabbi. He and his wife, Shirley, led the religious educational programming as well.

Shirley recalls the experience. In a "building not much bigger than your standard suburban home," she would "teach in the back of the synagogue, somebody would teach in front, and somebody would teach in the kitchen."[12] Members eschewed formal attire for jeans. Some farmers would arrive in boots, dungarees, and cowboy shirts.

The small Jewish community integrated into the town's larger population. For example, many synagogue members were active leaders on various civic boards.

But most of their children decided to leave the small town once they were grown. Some explain the demise of the local Jewish community as related to the degradation of the middle class, white flight, and a crisis among small, family-run farms. The agricultural landscape also changed from vegetable production to sugar cane production, which adversely impacted local Jewish farmers who did not operate in that sphere.

Those of the proceeding generation preferred conventional professions over merchant-class employment. Mark Greenberg paraphrased a quotation from Southern Jewish writer Eli Evans: "The history of the Jewish South is the history of fathers who built businesses for sons who didn't want them."[13]

Ultimately, the synagogue was down to three families. Beth

Sholom was seeing its final days. In 2000, it was sold to a Latino church. Members were happy that the building would still be a place of worship. The temple's prayer books and other artifacts were donated to congregations who needed them.

The few remaining members pray at Temple Beth El in West Palm Beach.

West Palm Beach

Temple Israel of West Palm Beach
1901 N Flagler Drive
Phone: (561) 833-8421
Website: www.temple-israel.com

One of the oldest temples in the region, Temple Israel started in 1923 with six Jewish families. Early members donated a lot for a building site on Broward Avenue. Founded as Temple Beth Israel, it was housed at 2020 Broward. The nascent congregation provided worship and social functions. The congregation increased to forty-five families during the real estate boom in the mid-1920s.

But then two hurricanes in 1926 and 1928 impeded momentum. The congregation could not meet its mortgage payments. The president implored Mrs. Nathan Spingold for help raising money. She obliged. The rear of the temple is named in her parents' honor.

Temple Israel grew through the 1930s. By the onset of World War II, its congregants were adversely impacted. Several congregants' sons were sent off to Europe to fight. In turn, the temple hosted Jewish soldiers serving in the army hospital at the Breakers Hotel. The Sisterhood of the Temple played a key part in the at-home war effort. They provided medical support and planned events like Shabbat dinners for army personnel so they would not feel isolated. Their goal was for "every Jewish solider stationed in the area to find a home away from home."[14]

After the war, the local economy surged, the population increased, and a larger building was needed. In August 1950, the congregation opened its new facility at 1901 N Flagler Drive. It offered rooms typically associated with synagogues: office spaces, a rabbi's study, a music room, a youth lounge, and classrooms. Eventually, the congregation split into Temple Israel and Temple Beth El, which was housed nearby at 2815 N Flagler Drive.

In 1991, the sanctuary was renovated with new symbolism. The bimah was on the eastern wall so worshippers could face Jerusalem. The ceiling was repainted to resemble biblical tents of ancestors. It embodied the quotation, "How lovely are your tents, O Jacob, your dwelling places, O Israel." Stained glass windows were added and the text from the Shima prayer was carved in Jerusalem stone. Years later, the congregation added an "Eternal Light" an "airy new ceiling to allow colored light to gently filter through."[15]

Members from the now-defunct Temple Beth Shalom in the small town of nearby Belle Glade worship here. The building was badly damaged by Hurricane Wilma in 2005 but has since been repaired.

Pedestrian Destinations
West Palm Beach

Clematis Street

The first Jews arrived in West Palm Beach in the late 1890s after Henry Flagler's transformational railroad was built. Many of these early Jews, like Isidor Cohen and Jake Schneidman, were merchants on Clematis Street in downtown West Palm Beach. Stores were close to the ferry that shuttled customers from the island. The area was populated by workers serving the opulent nearby Palm Beach. On this street was where early Jewish pioneers in the 1920s opened their retail stores, including the following:

- Joseph Schupler's hat store—opened by Joseph Schupler in 1915
- Cy Argintar's Men's Shop
- Toby and Selma Myers' luggage business (at 210 Clematis)
- Joseph Mendel's cigar manufacturing
- Shrebnick clothing
- Pioneer Linen (329 Clematis)[16]

Many of these merchants grouped their resources and started Temple Beth Israel in 1923, which later became Temple Israel of West Palm Beach. Yet many of the early merchants left for the Miami area. Max Serkin, a produce broker, was among the few

Founders of Brown's Diner, Harry and Florence Brown, were the first Jews in Boca Raton in 1931. (From the collections of the Jewish Museum of Florida-FIU, originated by Marcia Jo Zerivitz, founding executive director.)

Jack's Juice Bar opened by Jack Solomon in West Palm Beach in 1949. (From the collections of the Jewish Museum of Florida-FIU, originated by Marcia Jo Zerivitz, founding executive director.)

who remained. His daughter is said to have been the first known Jewish child born in the county. But the region's hurricanes stopped much of the development. The merchants lost considerable merchandise. One pioneer, Virginia Argintar, remarked, "One day I was riding in a limousine, the next day I waited for the bus."[17]

Today, you can visit the vestiges of that neighborhood. Stroll down this historic area of downtown West Palm Beach. It's known locally for its night clubs, live music, restaurants, and historic landmarks.

Other Museums and Cultural Attractions

These sites are not explicitly Jewish per this book's theme. Yet they are essential in the story of the area's development. The Flagler Museum was the home of one the region's most influential developers. The Juniper Lighthouse offers a compelling history of the area.

Flagler Museum
1 Whitehall Way
Phone: (561) 655-2833
Website: www.flaglermuseum.us
Hours: Tues.-Sat., 10 a.m.-5 p.m.; Sun., 12 p.m.-5 p.m.
Admission: Adults $18

Of the historic houses built by Gilded Age industrialists in the area, this one is probably the most famous. The history of South Florida is closely linked to Henry Flagler.

Henry Flagler's railroad transformed South Florida from a desolate and remote area. Speculators and developers followed. By the 1920s, newcomers flocked to the region.

In some ways, Flagler personified the American dream. Born to a reverend, he started working at the ripe age of fourteen. With his cousins, he worked in a grain store in a small town in Ohio for $5 per month plus room and board.

His first business venture was a failure. During the Civil War, Flagler and his brother-in-law, Barney York, created a salt company. It seemed like a solid investment given that Union soldiers needed salt for preservatives.

But the Civil War ended within a few years, and, with it, the need for salt greatly diminished. The company collapsed. Flagler was deep in debt.

Distressed but not out, Flagler turned back to the grain business and repaid his debts. He met the famed John D. Rockefeller, who was just starting to think about the oil business. Rockefeller badly needed capital; for that, he turned to Flagler. Borrowing funds from a relative, Flagler agreed. In doing so, he became a key equity partner. Soon, the Standard Oil Company was born. It would become the leader of the flourishing American oil refining industry.

Like the Weiss family in Miami Beach and many others, Flagler became acquainted with Florida on the advice of a doctor. His wife, Mar, was an invalid. Their physician hoped the new climate would alleviate her illness. Sadly, it did not. After her death, Flagler remarried and traveled to St. Augustine, Florida.

Flagler had an insight. The state, he believed, could be a key tourist destination, but it lacked the infrastructure. He built the Hotel Ponce de Leon—but that wasn't enough. A fundamental transition had to take place in transportation. He foresaw that this could open up remote southern parts of the state.

The Florida East Coast Railway system was born. Flagler's hotel empire expanded with his railway. By 1896, he built the famed Palm Beach Inn, which became the Breakers in 1901, in Palm Beach.

His railway reached the Biscayne Bay by 1896. Miami was changed forever. Residents wanted to name it after Flagler, but he declined, opting instead for an ancient Indian name for the river the settlement was built around—Miama.

By 1902, Flagler completed Whitehall, his winter home in Palm Beach. The *New York Herald* exclaimed that it was "more wonderful than any palace in Europe, grander and more magnificent than any other private dwelling in the world."[18] His architects were John Carrere and Thomas Hastings, who had designed one of Flagler's previous hotels and the New York Public Library. He and his wife, Mary Lily Kenan Flagler, used the opulent home as their winter retreat from 1902 until Flagler's death in 1913.

A few years after the building's completion, Flagler took on the "most ambitious engineering feat ever undertaken by a private citizen."[19] His Over-Sea Railroad to the populous Key West was completed. This allowed South Florida, and Key West in particular, to participate in trade with the rest of the country. When he visited Key West upon the Over-Sea Railroad's completion in 1912, Flagler was greeted with a hero's welcome.

Despite his staggering success, Flagler's end was near. Just a year after his Key West visit, he fell down a flight of stairs and died of his injuries a few months later.

After this tragedy, Whitehall's future was in doubt. It remained closed for about three years. Flagler's widow, Mary Lily, visited only once more with her new husband, Robert Bingham. She died shortly thereafter. Mary Lily bequeathed the house to her niece, Louise Lewis.

The house then underwent a fundamental change. Lewis sold it to investors who expanded it and converted the inside into a hotel. They added an eleven-story tower on the west side, which included hotel rooms, shops, and an immense penthouse on the top floor. Gala dinners and shows were held twice a week, and a variety of amenities were available to guests. The hotel operated for about thirty-five years, surviving the Great Depression and the country's entry into World War II. While Jews were restricted from many hotels, Whitehall allowed their patronage.

In the late 1950s, the opulent house was once again in jeopardy; the owners were considering demolishing it. Henry Flagler's granddaughter, Jean Flagler Matthews, formed a nonprofit corporation to save it called the Henry Morrison Flagler Museum.

The museum soon acquired Flagler's private railcar no. 91, a key part of his story. He traveled in this car to observe the completion of the railroad he envisioned, a railroad that forever changed the state.

Whitehall's façade is said to be designed to look like a temple to Apollo where muses would reside. The surrounding grounds were left to nature's devices. This is considered a reference to the "untamed bacchanalian world found outside the well-ordered world of the gods and muses inside the temple."[20] Inside the grand hall is a ceiling painting portraying the Oracle of Delphi. In Athens, the oracle was known for speaking the wise words "know thyself."

The interior of Whitehall is meant to uplift and inspire just as similar imagery would have the ancient Greeks. Another message, conveyed through Flagler's portrait, is that Flagler was a key leader of both business and of society.

Exterior and interior of Henry Flagler's estate in Palm Beach, also called Whitehall. When it was built in 1902, the New York Herald *declared the estate as "more wonderful than any palace in Europe, grander and more magnificent than any other private dwelling in the world." (© Flagler Museum.)*

Tips for the Traveler: Take the guided tour and explore the museum and its grounds. There is also a rotating exhibition gallery that features exhibitions related to Florida's history and the Gilded Age. Flagler was a key member of Gilded Age society, so in these exhibits you will learn about the larger societal context in which he prospered. Permanent exhibits focus on Flagler's life.

Visit Flagler's private railcar, railcar no. 91, situated in a nineteenth century Beaux Arts-style railway palace.

December is a special time to visit. The first floor and exterior are decorated in Gilded Age holiday splendor with electrical lights.

If you like music, make sure to see the 1,249-pipe organ in the music room and the Steinway Model B art case piano in the drawing room. On Sundays during specific times of the year, listen to a piano and organ concert of music that was popular during the period in which Flagler lived.

Jupiter

Jupiter Inlet Lighthouse
500 Captain Armour's Way
Phone: (561) 747-8380
Website: http://www.jupiterlighthouse.org
Hours: May–December, Tues.–Sun., 10 a.m.-5 p.m.
January–April, open seven days a week, 10 a.m.-5 p.m.

At this little-known museum is a chance to climb to the top of an 1860 lighthouse. You can learn about the South Florida area before it was developed at this waterfront history museum, which recounts the past five thousand years of the land. Other highlights are the "restored 1892 Tindall Pioneer Homestead exhibit, the 100-year old Pennock Plantation Bell, native plants and habitats, and the Keeper's Deck and Workshop under an historic ficus tree."[21]

If you would like a more in-depth experience, try one of the Lighthouse Education and Natural Sciences (LENS) tours like Hike through History. There's also an evening tour called Sunset and Moonrise.

Be sure not to miss the homemade fudge at the museum gift shop.

Notable Eateries

Boca Raton

Ben's
9942 Clint Moore Road
Phone: (561) 470-9963
Website: http://www.bensdeli.net

Ben's is a fun deli prominent in the New York City and Long Island areas. This location opened in more recent years.

In business since the early 1970s, the restaurant has always had the same owner and name—quite an accomplishment particularly in the cutthroat restaurant business.

Owner Ronnie Dragoon's father, Ben, was struggling in the dry-cleaning business. So he decided to work in delis, which were a key part of the Jewish New York culinary scene at the time. By the early 1970s, he opened his own Ben's Deli on West 72nd Street. Ben's son, Ronnie, opened his own deli on Long Island. He reinvested any spare change into the business. Within years, he opened several other locations.

In the mid-1990s, Ronnie seized on the opportunity to capture a respected venue on 38th Street in New York. It was above all a branding opportunity.

The Boca Raton branch has the same menu as the locations in Queens and Long Island. It has the usual deli fare of overstuffed sandwiches, smoked fish platters, homemade soups, and specialty dishes.

Part of the fun of eating at Ben's is the humorous quotations adorned around the restaurant:

"Yesterday's favorites homemade today."
"We cure our own beef. Chicken noodle soup cures everything else."
"At Ben's, we know everything about cold cuts and nothing about short cuts."
"When Ben's makes your buffet, make sure you have a strong table."
"Who said nosh can't be posh?"[22]

Browse the restaurant and read more.

Caketory
Del Mar Shopping Center
7160 Beracasa Way
Phone: (561) 672-7606
Website: www.facebook.com/caketorybocaraton

Caketory is a family-owned and operated kosher Pareve bakery. Browse the large selection of cakes, cookies, and breads. Customers especially like their chocolate cakes. There are also items for the shopper with lactose allergies.

Mozart Café
7300 W Camino Real Road
Phone: (561) 367-3412
Website: www.mozartcafebocaraton.com

This Boca Raton kosher dairy establishment seeks to "expand the boundaries of the Kosher dining experience, showcasing the casual gourmet creation and café bistro culture of the new Israeli cuisine."[23] The food selection varies from vegetarian dishes and salads to pizza. In this informal restaurant, "the outdoors wrap-around terraces seating offers view of gorgeous pools, fountains, and palm trees. At night drop the pools and trees lighting sparkles creating an ambiance of charm and magic."[24] Try the three-color mousse cake for dessert.

Orchid's Garden
9045 La Fontana Boulevard #109
Phone: (561) 482-3831
Website: www.orchidsgardenorb.com

This kosher Chinese restaurant offers many classic Chinese American dishes. If you dine in, you are treated to a complimentary dish of fried noodles and tea.

Boynton Beach

Flakowitz Bakery and Deli Restaurant
7410 W Boynton Beach Boulevard
Phone: (561) 742-4144
Website: http://www.flakowitzofboynton.com/

Open for over fifty years, this old-fashioned New York deli-style restaurant serves much of the traditional deli cuisine. It's been featured on food shows about diners and dives. Try some of the baked goods, as Flakowitz is not only a restaurant but also a bakery.

West Palm Beach

Sweet Endings (wholesale)
1220 Okeechobee Road
Phone: (561) 209-1907
Website: www.sweetendingsdesserts.com

This gourmet kosher-dairy dessert company offers one hundred deserts wholesale, including big boy layer cake, gourmet chocolate, and creamy cheesecakes. There is not a retail location, but you can order online for any occasion.

Sweet Endings was started by Judy Leibovit, a pastry chef. In the mid-1990s. she sold cakes to local restaurants and clubs from her car. She worked out of a rented kitchen in Temple Israel in West Palm Beach, one of the first synagogues in the area. Today, her product line has "over 90 cakes, tarts, pies, torts, cupcakes and brownies as well as special occasion cakes."[25]

Palm Beach

Too Jay's Original Gourmet Deli
313 Royal Poinciana Way
Phone: (561) 659-7232
Website: www.toojays.com

Started in 1981 on the island of Palm Beach, Too Jay's Original Gourmet Deli is a New York-style deli with huge sandwiches, soups, and classic desserts. It also offers salads, seasonal specialties, and a plethora of vegetarian options. It serves breakfast, lunch, and dinner, will deliver, and also offers catering. Today, there are locations throughout the state of Florida, with many in Palm Beach County.

Chapter Six

Snapshot Profiles

This section briefly describes Jewish individuals key to South Florida history. Each represents a different period. David Levy Yulee, the first Jewish member of the US senate, was a controversial yet enterprising figure in the pioneer days of Florida. Rose Weiss, the Mother of Miami Beach, was central to the city's development in its incipient decades. Barbara Capitman, through her architectural preservation efforts, represents a different time— the 1970s, when the area was in decline and its cultural heritage was in jeopardy. Phillip Frost is a contemporary philanthropist behind some of the area's revival and cultural institutions like the Museum of Science.

Then there are famous Jewish figures associated with New York City but who also have significant ties to South Florida. Irving Berlin wrote idyllic songs about the area. Bess Myerson built the inter-building pavilion at the Jewish Museum of Florida.

David Levy Yulee (1810-1886)

David Levy Yulee is probably best known as the first Jewish member of the United States Senate. He was also a prominent businessman, having founded the Florida Railroad Company. He was called the Father of Florida Railroads.

David Levy added "Yulee" to his name. It was from his Moroccan ancestry. Yulee converted to Christianity and raised his family as such. Nonetheless, he endured anti-Semitism throughout his political and business career. His attitudes aligned to those of the South at the time, as he supported slavery and was a fierce proponent of secession.

Whereas Yulee's temperament was practical and politically convenient, his father, Moses Levy, was more visionary. With some of the fortune he made in the lumber industry, Levy purchased fifty thousand acres of land near Jacksonville, Florida, to build a "New Jerusalem" for Jewish settlers. Despite his early efforts, the settlement was not fruitful in the long run.

David served in the military in the Second Seminole War and was later elected to Florida Territory's Legislative Council, where he served for four years. He was a huge proponent of statehood and lent a hand in drafting the state's constitution. In 1845, he was elected to the US Senate. He was not reelected, however.

In business, Yulee owned a prosperous sugar cane plantation. Slaves were a key part of his operation. Like Henry Flagler, who would come after him, he saw the development of infrastructure and the railroad as vital to the nascent state's future. He chartered the Florida Railroad in 1853. Yulee also fought for the expansion of slavery in new states. When the Civil War broke out, he was squarely on the Confederacy's side. An ardent supporter of slavery, he was impassioned when advocating for the institution. Nicknamed Florida Fire Eater, he is said to have spent the war years "tending his plantations and protecting his railroad."[1]

After the Civil War, he was jailed at Fort Pulaski for nine months for his participation in the Confederate cause, but he was later pardoned. After being released, he focused on his railroad. The business was failing financially, and he was forced to sell his majority share. Still, he is looked at in history as the Father of Florida Railroads.

He retired with his wife to Washington, DC, where he died six years later. Today, there are two municipalities named for him: Yulee, Florida, and Levy County, Florida.

Rose Weiss (1885-1974)

Rose Weiss is called the Mother of Miami Beach. Her devotion to civic life and to the city's development was legendary.

Born in Russia in the 1880s, she lived under the reign of an oppressive Czar. Her family did what many Jews in Russia dreamed of: immigrating to the US. They escaped through the Warsaw area. Weiss recounted the ordeal, describing how they left urgently and had little to eat other than the black bread, cheese, and herring they carried. Her family arrived in New York in 1892. It was a period of great Jewish immigration.

A state census in 1905 lists her as a seamstress. She later married Jeremiah Weiss. By 1920, she moved to the newly founded Miami Beach. A sufferer of asthma, her doctors advised the change in climate would suit her well. She, her husband, and their three children were among the city's first Jewish settlers.

After the Great Hurricane of 1926, Weiss distributed supplies and food to neglected residents. Once the area recovered, she turned her attention to civic maters. Weiss was key in creating Miami Beach's welfare department in the late 1920s. She developed the symbols and images of the city, too, and submitted the idea for its slogan: Forward with Caution. Like a Betsy Ross of Miami Beach, she designed the city's flag. In addition, Weiss organized the first Red Cross and sold $5 million in war bonds. She is said to have outsold any other woman in Florida.

Remarkably, she is said to have attended every council meeting for forty years. Never elected herself, she was referred to as the eighth councilman.

Elected officials actively sought her advice. One of Miami Beach's mayors, Chuck Hall, said of her, "She always had her finger on the pulse of the people."[2]

Her children recount how she was somewhat strict in standards of dress and decorum. They note that she "made it clear that she disapproved of women wearing trousers and smoking in public."[3]

Weiss was friendly with Carl Fisher, the visionary of Miami Beach. He is said to have remarked that it was "his money and her spirit that built the city."[4]

Rose Weiss Park at the corner of Washington Avenue and 2nd Street was named in her honor. Today the sign is gone, but memory of her deeds remains.

Meyer Lansky (1902-1983)

One of the best known Jewish mobsters, Meyer Lansky built a worldwide empire. He was said to own casinos in Las Vegas, Cuba, and parts of Europe and the Caribbean. He was referred to as the Mob's Accountant.

Lansky was born Meier Suchowlanski in the Russian Empire. As unfortunately was common, his family was victimized by pogroms or attacks from villagers. His family left Russia in 1911 and immigrated to the famed Lower East Side of New York City. At the time, it was the most densely populated neighborhood in the world. Teeming with immigrants from many areas, it was known for its crowded housing and poor conditions.

As a teenager, Lansky became acquainted with someone who would become one of his closest friends and business associates: Bugsy Siegel. Both Jewish immigrants from similar backgrounds, the two came of age as organized crime was flourishing under Prohibition. They formed the Bugs and Meyer Mob and often partnered with Lucky Luciano.

Lansky expanded his business to gambling operations in the mid-1930s, primarily out of South Florida, Cuba, and New Orleans. Though much of the gambling was illegal, it was said that the actual gaming was legitimate. Lansky made sure that his staff played the games fairly. Nothing was rigged.

Luciano did not enjoy the same success as his partners. In 1936, he was sentenced to prison time.

Luciano's sentence, as well as Al Capone's 1931 conviction for tax evasion, chilled mobsters. They felt they too could be indicted, so they placed all illegal earnings in a Swiss bank account protected by the 1934 Swiss Banking Act. This played a key role in money laundering.

Lansky was not only concerned with building his empire but also with key political causes. During the turbulent 1930s, he is said to have disrupted Nazi rallies in New York's Upper East Side. He described the scene of one: "The stage was decorated with a swastika and a picture of Adolf Hitler. The speakers started ranting. There were only fifteen of us, but we went into action. We threw some of them out the windows. Most of the Nazis panicked and ran out. We chased them and beat them up. We wanted to show them that Jews would not always sit back and accept insults."[5]

During World War II, his skills came in handy for assisting the Office of Naval Intelligence. He was able to help identify enemy positions from covert positions. He and his team also struck a deal with the US government to provide security for military ships in exchange for Luciano's shortened prison time.

Changes in the political landscape did not bode well for Lansky. In 1960, Castro's government took control of casinos and made

GENEROUS CONTRIBUTOR
MEYER LANSKY

*Stained glass window at Congregation Beth Jacob, now
the Jewish Museum of Florida, honoring Meyer Lansky's
contributions.* (Photo by Aaron Davidson.)

gambling illegal. Much of Lansky's wealth was wiped out. He lost more with additional casino closures, the result of government crackdowns in Miami.

Lansky had always been a strong supporter of Israel. He fled there to avoid tax evasion charges. A few years later, though, he was deported back to the United States to face trial. He was acquitted. Lansky felt that he had helped Israel a great deal and objected strongly to their decision not to grant him citizenship.

Lansky died in Miami Beach from lung cancer in 1983 at the age of eighty. His wealth at the time of his death is disputable. Some accounts peg his real wealth at the time at $300 million. Still, those close to him say his assets were far less. There is also speculation that he lost most of his wealth with the changes in Cuba during the 1960s and 1970s. His true fortune will likely never be known.

The characters of Hyman Roth and Michael Corleone in *The Godfather: Part II* are based loosely on Lansky.

Barbara Capitman (1921-1990)

Today, a street in South Beach stands in Barbara Capitman's name as a testament to her architectural preservation efforts. She turned around Miami Beach during its decline by changing the public perception of the value of architecture to the landscape. At a time when hotel landlords were ignoring their properties, she showed Miami Beach why their architecture was worth saving. She transformed a dilapidated area of Miami Beach into a colorful art deco historic district. In doing so, she helped revamp the fledgling city.

Capitman felt a deep link to art deco. She once said, "My whole life had been art deco. I was born at the beginning of the period and grew up during the height of it. It's a thing of fate."[6]

After a career in advertising and as a reporter, she moved to Miami Beach in 1973. Three years later, Capitman founded the Miami Design Preservation League to arrest the destruction of architecturally historic buildings. She was successful organizationally if not socially. Her "outspoken, unorthodox manner led to her ouster from the group."[7] One of her achievements was getting the South Beach District on the National Register of

Historic Places to bring tax relief and other benefits. The most important result was protecting the art deco buildings from demolition.

Capitman helped found chapters of the Art Deco Society in other US cities. She partnered with industrial designer Leonard Horowitz to beautify the area. Horowitz convinced landlords to let their hotel facades be painted in brighter, more appealing colors.

In 1988, Capitman's book, *Deco Delights: Preserving the Beauty and Joy of Miami Beach Architecture*, was published.

She died in 1990 at the age of sixty-nine. A stretch of 10th Street between Washington Avenue and Ocean Drive was renamed for her.

Phillip Frost (1936–present)

Frost began life as the son of a shoe store owner. He would eventually earn a fortune of $2.4 billion, becoming one of the wealthiest men in the United States by developing and selling pharmaceutical companies. He also is one of the nation's great philanthropists. He and his wife, Patricia, are major donors to cultural museums in Miami-Dade County, And he has pledged to give away $1 billion more.

Frost grew up above a shoe shop in an Italian market in South Philadelphia. His family was Jewish by religion. His father was fond of Yiddish songs. After attending the University of Pennsylvania, Frost considered medical school but balked at the high tuition. He ran into a high school classmate who mentioned a full scholarship for alumni of their school to the Albert Einstein College of Medicine in New York City. Frost was awarded the scholarship and specialized in dermatology research.

By the mid-1960s, he ended up on the faculty at the University of Miami. At this time, the civil rights movement was heating up. Patricia Frost was instrumental in efforts to integrate schools. The couple found themselves playing a role in the movement.

Frost was to be a professor, but he found himself constantly thinking of business ideas. He started to realize he was more of an entrepreneur than an academic. Constrained by the university, he changed tracks to join the Mount Sinai Medical Center in Miami

Beach and took charge of the emerging dermatology department.

By the mid-1970s, Frost was embracing innovative medical and dental products. For example, he purchased a dental firm that utilized ultrasound to clean teeth. Frost partnered with a New York pharmaceutical lawyer named Mike Jaharis and convinced him to leave his large employer to start a health care company. The pair collaborated with a fledgling drug manufacturer, Key Pharmaceuticals. Key was in serious financial trouble. It also had an untested product. Its turnaround, though, was stunning. By tweaking its asthma product to become a time-release capsule, sales rose.

By the mid-1980s, Frost has become one of the wealthiest men in the United States. He built other companies, noting that his preference was to "build not to manage."[8] Later, he developed IVAX, another pharmaceutical company, which was eventually purchased by the Israeli company Teva Pharmaceutical.

Philip and Patricia Frost are avid art collectors. They gave away many paintings to the Smithsonian. When they moved to Star Island in 2001, they hired Italian craftsmen to install several types of stone in their house. They donated to the University of Miami Music School and the new Miami Museum of Science. Philip Frost also signed the famous pledge created by Warren Buffet and Bill Gates to donate half his fortune.

Irving Berlin (1888-1989)

Famed songwriter Irving Berlin wrote two famous songs about the Sunshine State. The first, "In Florida Among the Palms," was introduced in 1916 in the show *Ziegfield Follies*.

At that time, Miami Beach was undeveloped and Miami was still a small city. Much of the area was rural. Still, the song is nostalgic and longing for a "sunny South." It idealizes the laid-back atmosphere. "Its peaceful air of 'I don't care' and lazy atmosphere that calms. I'd love to live among the bamboo huts, the cocoanuts . . ."

In 1925, he wrote "Florida by the Sea" for the Marx Brothers musical *The Cocoanuts*. The song is a product of the time in which it was written. Visiting or moving to Florida was idealized. Properties were selling rapidly. Speculation was rampant. The song notes a million "million dollar nuts" will be found, perhaps referring to the land-grabbing. It later says, "Buy a lot, any piece that we've got will increase ev'ry season," clearly referring to the real estate promise that the value of land in Florida in the mid-1920s could only rise.

Of course, the opposite happened. Only one year later, the Great Hurricane of 1926 hit and threw the area into a depression. The market crashed. The song was not a great prognosticator.

Irving Berlin is considered one of the great songwriters. He was surely one of the most prolific. Astoundingly, he never learned to read or write music. Dropping out of school at age fourteen, he was self-taught. He was said to only know the black keys. Few knew about his piano lever trick—he played on a piano with a lever underneath it. He would shift the lever, changing the tones to suit the particular song or performer.

Berlin was the personification of the American Dream. Born in 1888 as Israel Baline to a poor Jewish family in a small town in the Russian Empire, his family escaped to the freedom of the US when he was only five. His family settled in a crowded tenement in the Lower East Side. His siblings toiled in factory jobs.

At fourteen, he left home for the rough neighborhood streets. He worked in saloons, where he taught himself the piano. He began to write a few hit songs and was noted at the music publishing center Tin Pan Alley (which was given that name because pianos were constantly playing, sounding like banging on tin pans in an alleyway).

Berlin became quite famous from his song "Alexander's Ragtime Band." He was later drafted into the army. He was not a good fit for it, but he realized how to succeed in it—by composing music. He wrote a satirical play about military life called *Yip Yip Yaphank* with the song "Oh, How I Hate to Get Up in the Morning."

He also wrote "God Bless America" but shelved it, believing it to be too corny. Yet, twenty years later, times changed. The nation was yet again at the brink of war. The song took on a new life, so Berlin released it. Performed by Kate Smith, it became an informal national anthem.

Berlin also wrote music for Broadway musicals like *Annie Get Your Gun* and *Call Me Madam*, as well as for films like *Top Hat*,

There's No Business Like Show Business, and *White Christmas*. In total, he wrote a staggering 1,500 songs throughout his life.

Irving Berlin lived to be 101 years old. Yet he was said to be in self-imposed exile during his final two decades. He largely stayed in his New York apartment with his wife and had virtually no outside contact. He declined to watch a national TV broadcast from Carnegie Center honoring him on his one hundredth birthday. Still, his songs like "White Christmas," "Easter Parade," "Puttin' on the Ritz," "Blue Skies," and "God Bless America" are American classics.

Bess Myerson (1924-2014)

In the Jewish Museum of Florida on 3rd Street in South Beach, you will notice Bessie's Bistro. Once two separate buildings belonging to the area's first Jewish congregation, they are now adjoined by a sky-lighted center court. The area was to be a bistro. Today, it's a self-service snack area. This court and bistro were funded by Myerson. She felt a connection to the area as her parents lived in the neighborhood.

Myerson is best known for being the only Jewish Miss America, crowned in 1945. She grew up in the Bronx, New York, in a working-class family. She said she felt awkward as a teenager, but in high school her beauty was noticed by all. She attended New York's Hunter College and was studying music when a photographer heard about a competition for Miss New York City. He consulted her sister Sylvia. Knowing that Bess was likely to say no, they entered her in the contest without telling her.

At the pageant, she received pressure to change her name so it would sound less Jewish. She refused. She was also told that many sponsors threatened to pull out if she won, as they objected to a Jewish Miss America.

Win Meyerson did. She became an instant celebrity and won $5,000, a small fortune at the time. Her name was mentioned everywhere. On national tour as Miss America, she encountered significant anti-Semitism.

Later, she became an actress and was a frequent guest on the celebrity quiz show *I've Got a Secret*. She also joined New York City politics as a commissioner and eventually unsuccessfully ran

Bess Myerson, the first Jewish Miss America, who was crowned in 1945.
(From the collections of the Jewish Museum of Florida-FIU, originated
by Marcia Jo Zerivitz, founding executive director.)

for US Senate. By the late 1980s, she was indicted on a bribery
and corruption charge. Though she was acquitted, her reputation
was in tatters. It was known as the Bess Mess.

In the 1990s and 2000s, Meyerson returned to private life. She
became active with the Jewish Museum of Florida and donated
funds for the pavilion in the museum that connects the two
buildings.

Meyerson died in December 2014.

Suggested Videos

History of Jews in Miami Beach Told by a Docent at the Jewish Museum of Florida

http://www.youtube.com/watch?v=Gz97CLYao9E

Momma Lives on Miami Beach, 1974: A TV Documentary Looks at the Life of the Elderly

http://www.youtube.com/watch?v=3P9RJcIWekA
http://www.youtube.com/watch?v=1fOszxGYtVY
http://www.youtube.com/watch?v=AnIb_cwcOAs
http://www.youtube.com/watch?v=g9n_qGCX8B0
http://www.youtube.com/watch?v=53bkFXoMJ-c

Jewish Contributors to Lincoln Road Mall

http://www.youtube.com/watch?v=M3TW8dtHxHQ

Jewish Museum of Florida

http://cityvideoinfo.com/Miami/Jewish-Museum-of-Florida/9062

Rascal House Deli, Miami Beach

http://www.youtube.com/watch?v=bnHVWW98VbQ

Miami Beach Crackdown on Jaywalking, 1970: Great Slice of Life Scenes in Three Parts

http://www.youtube.com/watch?v=bJ_UmNbicx4
http://www.youtube.com/watch?v=6zAH1XYCEd0
http://www.youtube.com/watch?v=z-45nwGKosI

Where Neon Goes to Die:[1] About Yiddish Theater in Miami Beach

http://www.youtube.com/watch?v=bUaspHjKQBY

Notes

Chapter One: History of Jews in South Florida

1. Sol Beton, "Columbus and the Jewish connection," sefarad.org/sefarad/sefarad.php/id/55/.

2. Lisa J. Huriash, "Some Hispanics feel mysterious tug of Jewish heritage," *Sun Sentinel*, www.sun-sentinel.com/fl-spanish-jews-20100614-story.html.

3. Henry Green and Marcia Zerivitz, *Mosaic: Jewish Life in Florida* (Coral Gables, FL: Mosaic, 1991), 8.

4. Bob Blythe, "Haym Salomon (ca. 1740-1785)," The American Revolution: Lighting Freedom's Flame, www.nps.gov/revwar/about_the_revolution/haym_salomom.html.

5. Green and Zerivitz, *Mosaic*, 9.

6. C.S. Monaco, *Moses Levy of Florida, Jewish Utopian and Antebellum Reformer* (Baton Rouge: Louisiana State University Press, 2005),105.

7. Leon Hühner, "David Yulee, Florida's First Senator," Publications of the American Jewish Historical Society, No. 25 (1917), 15.

8. Malvina Liebman and Seymour Liebman, *Jewish Frontiersman* (Miami Beach: Jewish Historical Society of South Florida), 13.

9. Jefferson B. Browne, *Key West: The Old and the New St. Augustine* (The Record Co., 1912), 24.

10. Liebman and Liebman, *Jewish Frontiersman*, 17.

11. Isidor Cohen, "Historical Sketches and Sidelights of Miami, Florida," private printer, 1925.

12. Green and Zerivitz, *Mosaic*, 25.

13. Exhibit on Miami Beach history at Wolfsonian Museum-FIU, 2015.

14. Marcia Kerstein Zerivitz, *Alligators and Matzo Balls: A Historical Overview of the Florida Jewish Community* (Brandeis University Press, 2005), 23.

15. Liebman and Liebman, *Jewish Frontiersman*, 36.

16. Ibid, 40.

17. Zerivitz, *Alligators and Matzo Balls*, 30.

18. Deborah Dash Moore, *To the Golden Cities: Pursuing the American Dream in Miami and LA* (New York: Free Press, 1994), 155.

19. Personal correspondence dated February 13, 1929. Collection of the Historical Association of Southern Florida, Inc.

20. Richard Nagler, *My Love Affair with Miami Beach* (New York: Simon and Schuster, 1991), 25.

21. Moore, "To the Golden Cities," 25

22. Ibid.

23. Zerivitz, *Alligators and Matzo Balls*, 20.

24. Ariella Siegel, "Why is This Wave Different from All Other Waves," *Jewish Miami: The Changing Face of Institutional Interaction in Three Phases*, Florida International University master's thesis, July 2012.

25. Ibid.

26. Dennis Eisenberg, *Meyer Lansky: Mogul of the Mob* (New York: Paddington, 1979), 319-20.

27. Stephen Benz, "Cuban Jews in South Florida: Exile Redux" (Brandeis University Press, 2005), 69.

28. Ibid.

29. www.allenmorris.com/crane-state-bird-florida.

30. Benz, "Cuban Jews in South Florida," 26.

31. Ibid, 18.

Chapter Two: Miami Beach

1. Miami Design Preservation League website and museum exhibits, mdpl.org.

2. Sara Churchville, "Miami Modern Architecture," *South Beach Magazine*, May 2004.

3. Jewish Museum of Florida-FIU, jmof.fiu.edu.

4. Ibid.

5. Ibid.

6. Miami Design Preservation League, mdpl.org.

7. "About," Wolfsonian-FIU, wolfsonian.org/about.

8. World Erotic Art Museum, weam.org.

9. WGBH on PBS, www.pbs.org/wgbh/amex/miami/sfeature/decomiamibeach.html.

10. "Architect: Henry Houser," Bric and Cornice, June 11, 2014, brickandcornice.com/architect-henry-hohauser.

11. Jennifer Rosenberg, "The History of the Balfour Declaration," ThoughtCo., last updated March 17, 2017, thoughtco.com/balfour-declaration-1778163.

12. Seth Sherwood, "Hotel Review: Lord Balfour in Miami Beach," February 28, 2014, http://www.nytimes.com/2014/03/02/travel/hotel-review-lord-balfour-in-miami-beach.html?_r=0).

13. Charlotte Hildebrand, "Ghosts on the Beach," *Jewish Journal*,

June 15, 2000, jewishjournal.com/culture/lifestyle/travel/2977.

14. Ibid.

15. Francisco Alvarado, "FBI probes claim of $130 million healthcare scam," November 23, 2014, *Miami Herald*, www.miamiherald.com/news/local/community/miami-dade/article4082187.html.

16. "Versace Mansion reopens as over-the-top luxury hotel in Miami," March 17, 2014, www.foxnews.com/travel/2014/03/17/versace-mansion-reopens-as-over-top-luxury-hotel-in-miami.

17. Joe's Stone Crab Restaurant, www.joesstonecrab.com.

18. Ibid.

19. Ibid.

20. Ibid.

21. Postcard entitled "The Brighter Side," Damon Runyon and King Features, circa 1940.

22. "About Us," Myles Restaurant Group, mylesrestaurantgroup.com/?page_id=239.

23. Howard Brayer's Miami Beach tour and notes.

24. Interview at Holocaust Memorial site, November 2015.

25. Holocaust Memorial, holocaustmemorialmiamibeach.org.

26. Ibid.

27. Ibid.

28. Ibid.

29. Hebrew Academy, http://www.rasg.org.

30. Eden Roc: Miami Beach Resort, edenrochotelmiami.com/en/home.

31. Fontainebleau Miami Beach, Fontainebleau.com.

32. Damien Cave, "A Deli Destination, Now a Pastrami-Scented Memory, *New York Times*, April 1, 2008, www.nytimes.com/2008/04/01/us/01miami.html?_r=0.

33. "Temple Menorah History," Temple Menorah Miami, templemenorahmiami.org/temple-menorah-history.

34. Ibid.

35. Temple Moses: Sephardic Congregation of Florida, www.templemoses.com.

36. Interview with Rabbi Daniel Hadar, Temple Moses.

37. Peter Zalewski, "Miami Beach's Deauville Condo-Hotel units to be terminated and sold," The Real Deal, December 14, 2016, therealdeal.com/miami/blog/2014/12/16/538-units-in-deauville-condo-hotel-miami-beach-to-be-sold-after-termination.

38. Ibid.

Chapter Three: Miami

1. Marcia Jo Zerivitz, *Jews of Greater Miami* (Charleston, SC: Arcadia, 2009), 8.

2. Demographic study, Greater Miami Jewish Federation, 2015.

3. Miami Museum of Science, miamisci.org.

4. Perez Museum of Art, pamm.org.

5. "Perez Art Museum Miami: Exhibitions Schedule 2014," April 4, 2014, pamm.org/about/news/2014/p%C3%A9rez-art-museum-miami-exhibitions-schedule-2014.

6. Clara Gillman, "Beth David Congregation: Centennial Celebration, 1912-2012" (Miami: Beth David Congregation, 2012).

7. Interview with Melody Torrens, executive vice president, Beth David Congregation.

8. Temple Israel, templeisrael.net.

9. Kenneth Treister, *Chapel of Light: Jewish Ceremonial Art in the Sophie and Nathan Gumenick Chapel* (New York: Union of American Hebrew Congregations, 2000), 16.

10. Ibid, 38.

11. Marvin Glassman, "Miami's Jewish history showcased in cemetery walking tout," *Sun Sentinel*, September 28, 2015, www.sun-sentinel.com/florida-jewish-journal/news/miami-dade/fl-jjdc-history-0923-20150928-story.html.

12. Paul S. George, *Little Havana: Images of America* (Charleston, SC: Arcadia Publishing), 7.

13. "Miami Walking Tour: Calle Ocho," National Geographic, travel.nationalgeographic.com/travel/city-guides/miami-walking-tour-3.

14. Greg Allen, "Amid Redevelopment Plans, Miami Residents Fight To Save Little Havana," NPR, October 6, 2015, http://www.npr.org/2015/10/06/446370821/amid-redevelopment-plans-miami-residents-fight-to-save-little-havana.

15. "Collections," HistoryMiami Museum, historymiami.org/collections/.

16. "Miami Stories," HistoryMiami Museum, historymiami.org/miamistories/.

17. One Minute Play Festival, oneminuteplayfestival.com.

18. Jackie Salo, "Are there ghosts at the Deering Estate? Check out the 'Spookover' and ghost tour," *Miami Herald*, October 13, 2014, miamiherald.com/news/local/community/miami-dade/palmetto-bay/article2702249.html.

19. Matt Meltzer, "Miami's Ten Best Delicatessens," Thrillist, August 20, 2015, www.thrillist.com/eat/miami/10-best-delis-in-miami-josh-s-deli-stephen-s-in-hialeah.

Chapter Four: Broward County

1. Press kit for the Holocaust Documentation and Education Center, Inc.

2. Ibid.

3. Ibid.

4. Brian Ballou, "Holocaust Documentation and Education Center getting ready to open in Dania Beach," *Sun Sentinel*, January 17, 2016, http://www.sun-sentinel.com/local/broward/fl-holocaust-museum-preview-20160117-story.html.

5. Ibid.

6. Rositta Kenigsberg, president of the Holocaust Documentation and Education Center.

7. Historic Needham Estate, historicneedhamestate.com/history.

8. Robert Nolin, "A cross-cultural 'ho ho ho' all year long," *Sun Sentinel*, March 3, 2015, sun-sentinel.com/local/broward/broward-centennial/fl-jewish-santa-brow100-20150308-story.html.

9. James D. David, "Temple Emanu-el Turns 75 Years Young," *Sun Sentinel*, March 17, 2001, articles.sun-sentinel.com/2001-03-17/news/0103160867_1_temple-emanu-el-temple-president-reform-temple.

10. Ibid.

11. Kevin Smith, "Synagogues Prepare For Merger: Worshipers, Rabbi To Join At Temple Kol Ami In Plantation," August 12, 2004, *Sun Sentinel*, articles.sun-sentinel.com/2004-08-12/news/0408120105_1_temple-emanu-el-county-s-largest-synagogue-new-temple

12. David A. Schwartz, "Synagogue celebrates 'double chai' anniversary," *Sun Sentinel*, May 9, 2012, http://articles.sun-sentinel.com/2012-05-09/news/fl-jjbs-ramat-0510-20120509_1_reconstructionist-synagogue-ramat-shalom-synagogue-torah.

13. Marcia Zerivitz and Rachel Heimovics, *Florida Jewish Heritage Trail* (Florida Department of State, Division of Historical Resources, 2000), 34.

14. Tao Woolfe and Ray Lynch, "The Lady of Bonnet House," *Sun Sentinel*, July 2, 1997, articles.sun-sentinel.com/1997-07-02/news/9707020014_1_frederic-bartlett-eli-lilly-bonnet-house.

15. Stuart McIver, "A House with Humor," *Sun Sentinel*, January 11, 1987, http://articles.sun-sentinel.com/1987-01-11/features/8701020531_1_historic-preservation-bonnet-house-house-lot.

16. Shireen Sandoval, "The Beautiful Bonnet House," WVSN-TV, April 1, 2015, wsvn.com/story/28697873/the-beautiful-bonnet-house.

17. Stranahan House, stranahanhouse.org.

18. "Frank & Ivy Stranahan—Founders of Fort Lauderdale," Florida Irish Heritage Center, May 23, 2010, floridairishheritagecenter.wordpress.com/2010/05/23/frank-ivy-stranahan-founders-of-fort-lauderdale.

19. Alejandra Cancino, "Stranahan House," *Sun Sentinel*, sun-sentinel.com/sfl-stranahanhistory-story.html.

20. NY Deli, nydeli.us.

21. Pomperdale deli, pomperdaledeli.us.

22. "Café Emunah," *Great Kosher Restaurants Magazine*, greatkosherrestaurants.com/restaurants/324/cafe-emunah.

23. "Hoffman Chocolates: From The Florida Tropics Comes A Really Hot Product," OU Kosher, December 25, 2006, oukosher.org/blog/corporate/hoffman-chocolates-from-the-florida-tropics-comes-a-really-hot-product.

Chapter Five: Palm Beach County

1. Norton Museum of Art, norton.org.

2. Interview with Shelly Isaacs.

3. Hap Erstein, "The Palm Beach Jewish Film Festival covers stories from Boca to Europe," myPalmBeachPost, January 18, 2016, http://www.mypalmbeachpost.com/news/entertainment/the-palm-beach-jewish-film-festival-covers-stories/np54G/.

4. Ibid.

5. Recorded Sound Archives: Judaica Collection, FAU Libraries, https://rsa.fau.edu/judaic.

6. Ibid.

7. Ibid.

8. Interview with Aaron Kula.

9. Ibid.

10. Larry Luxner, "The Jewish Traveler: Palm Beach," *Hadassah Magazine*, February 2007.

11. *Palm Beach Post* staff researchers, "'We went from being tolerated to being accepted to being respected,'" *Palm Beach Post*, September 12, 2007, historicpalmbeach.blog.palmbeachpost.com/2007/09/12/we-went-from-being-tolerated-to-being-accepted-to-being-respected.

12. Ibid.

13. Ibid.

14. "Our History," Temple Israel, temple-israel.com/about-us/our-history/55-our-history.

15. Temple Israel of West Palm Beach, temple-israel.com.

16. Marcia Zerivitz, *Florida Jewish Heritage Trail* (Florida Department of State, Division of Historical Resources, 2000), 33.

17. "Palm Beach County," Jewish Virtual Library: A Project of AICE," jewishvirtuallibrary.org/palm-beach-county.

18. "Welcome to the Flagler Museum," Henry Morrison Flagler Museum, flaglermuseum.us/10-general-public/general/1-welcome-to-the-flagler-museum.

19. "Henry Morrison Flagler Biography," flaglermuseum.us/history/flagler-biography.

20. "Whitehall," Henry Morrison Flagler Museum, https://www. flaglermuseum.us/history/whitehall.

21. Jupiter Light House, jupiterlighthouse.org.

22. Quotations are on the restaurant walls of Ben's in Boca Raton and on their website, bensdeli.net.

23. Mozart Café Boca Raton, manta.com.

24. Ibid.

25. "Bakery owner once worked from a car," *Sun Sentinel*, May 27, 2010, http://articles.sun-sentinel.com/2010-05-27/features/fl-food-chef-du-jour-052010-20100527_1_cakes-bakery-sweet-endings.

Chapter Six: Snapshot Profiles

1. Maury Wiseman, "David Levy Yulee: Conflict and Continuity in Social Memory," http://fch.fiu.edu/FCH-2006/Wiseman-David%20 Levy%20Yulee.htm.

2. docmgmt.miamibeachfl.gov/WebLink/DocView.aspx?dbid=0&id= 76435&page=3&cr=1.

3. Alexa Rossy, "From Pogroms to Palm Trees: Rose Weiss, 'The Mother of Miami Beach,'" HistoryMiami, historymiami.org/fastspot/ research-miami/miamistories/miami-stories/details/alexa-rossy/index. html.

4. Ibid.

5. "Jews in America: Jewish Gangsters," Jewish Virtual Library: A Project of AICE, jewishvirtuallibrary.org/jsource/US-Israel/gangsters. html.

6. Joan Cook, "Barbara Baer Capitman, 69, Dies; Created Miami Art Deco District," *New York Times*, March 31, 1990, nytimes. com/1990/03/31/obituaries/barbara-baer-capitman-69-dies-created-miami-art-deco-district.html.

7. Ibid.

8. "Billionaire Phillip Frost an 'entrepreneur's entrepreneur,'" Jewish Insider, January 6, 2013, jewishinsider.com/220/billionaire-phillip-frost-an-entrepreneurs-entrepreneur.

Appendix: Suggested Videos

1. From a phrase coined by comedian Lenny Bruce in describing Miami Beach.

References

Books

Bramson, Seth. *Sunshine, Stone Crabs and Cheesecake*. Charleston, SC: History Press, 2009.

Dworkin, Susan. *Miss America, 1945: Bess Myerson's Own Story*. New York: New Market Press, 1987.

Eisenberg, Dennis. *Meyer Lansky: Mogul of the Mob*. New York: Paddington Press, 1979.

George, Paul. *Little Havana, Images of America*. Charleston, SC: Arcadia Publishing, 2007.

Gillman, Clara. *Beth David Congregation: Centennial Celebration, 1912-2012*. Miami: Beth David Congregation, self-published, 2012.

Green, Henry and Marcia Zerivitz. *Mosaic: Jewish Life in Florida*. Coral Gables, FL: Mosaic, 1991.

Greenbaum, Andrea, ed. *Jews of South Florida*. Waltham, MA: Brandeis University Press, 2005.

Ferris, Marcie. *Matzoh Ball Gumbo: Culinary Tales of the Jewish South*. Raleigh: University of North Carolina Press, 2005.

Liebman, Malvina and Seymour Liebman. *Jewish Frontiersman*. Miami Beach: Jewish Historical Society of South Florida.

Moore, Deborah Dash. *To the Golden Cities: Pursuing the American Dream in Miami and LA*. New York: Free Press, 1994.

Nagler, Richard. *My Love Affair with Miami Beach*. New York: Simon and Schuster, 1991.

Tebeau, Charlton. *Synagogue in the Central City: Temple Israel of Greater Miami, 1922-1972*. Miami: University of Miami Press, 1972.

Treister, Kenneth. *Chapel of Light*. New York: Union of American Hebrew Congregations, 2000.

Zerivitz, Marcia and Rachel Heimovics. *Florida Jewish Heritage Trail*. Florida Department of State, Division of Historical Resources, 2000.

Articles

Benz, Stephen, "Cuban Jews in South Florida: Exile." Waltham, MA: Brandeis University Press, 2005.

Churchville, Sara. "Miami Modern Architecture." *South Beach Magazine,* May 2004.

Fromm, Annette. "Sephardic Jews in South Florida," in Greenbaum, Andrea, ed. *Jews of South Florida.* Waltham, MA: Brandeis University Press, 2005.

Hühner, Leon. "David Yulee, Florida's First Senator." Publications of the American Jewish Historical Society, No. 25, 15 (1917).

Luxner, Larry. "The Jewish Traveler: Palm Beach." *Hadassah Magazine,* February 2007.

Siegel, Ariella. "Why is This Wave Different from All Other Waves? Jewish Miami: The Changing Face of Institutional Interaction in Three Phases." Florida International University, master's thesis, July 2012.

Online Sources
fau.edu/jsa (Florida Atlantic University Libraries)
fontainebleau.com (Fontainebleau Miami Beach)
foxnews.com (Fox News)
historicneedhamestate.com/history (Historic Needham Estate)
historicpalmbeach.blog.palmbeachpost.com (Historic Palm Beach Blog)
holocaustmemorialmiamibeach.org (Holocaust Memorial Miami Beach)
jewishjournal.com (Jewish Journal)
jmof.fiu.edu (Jewish Museum of Florida-Florida International University)
joesstonecrab.com (Joe's Stone Crab)
jupiterlighthouse.org (Jupiter Inlet Lighthouse and Museum)
mdpl.org (Miami Design Preservation League)
miamisci.org (Miami Museum of Science)
miamiherald.com (Miami Herald)
mozartcafebocaraton.com (Mozart Café Boca Raton)
nationalgeographic.com (National Geographic)
newyorktimes.com (New York Times)
norton.org (Norton Museum of Art)
oneminuteplayfestival.com (One Minute Play Festival)
oukosher.org/blog/corporate/hoffman-chocolates-from-the-florida-tropics-comes-a-really-hot-product (OU Kosher: Hoffman Chocolates)
pbs.org (PBS)
pamm.org (Perez Museum of Art)
pomperdalenydeli.com (Pomperdale New York Deli)
stranahanhouse.org (Stranahan House Museum)
temple-israel.com (Temple Israel of West Palm Beach)
templemoses.com (Temple Moses)
thrilllist.com (Thrillist)
weam.org (World Erotic Art Museum)

Interview Subjects

Todd Bothel, registrar and curator of the Jewish Museum of Florida
Howard Brayer, tour guide of Miami Beach
Stephanie Cohen, director of educational outreach, the Holocaust Documentation and Education Center
Brian Goldstein, Goldstein's Prime
Paul George, professor at Miami-Dade College
Andy Gottliep, Temple Israel
Rabbi Daniel Hadar, Temple Moses
Rita Hofstradder, longtime volunteer at the Holocaust Documentation and Education Center
Shelly Issacs, Café Cinematheque
Rositta Kenigsberg, president of the Holocaust Documentation and Education Center
Aaron Kula, Florida Atlantic University Library Archives and Klezmer Company Orchestra
David Oakes, Kol Ami Congregation
Lida Shukrie, Holocaust Memorial
Melody Torrens, executive vice president of Beth David Congregation

Index

5th Street Gym, 70

Alper Jewish Community Center, 115
anti-Semitism, 22, 28, 199, 208
art deco, 40, 47-49, 51-52, 57-58, 61-64, 80-81, 204-5
Ashkenazi Jews, 9, 32

Bass Museum of Art, 89
Bay of Pigs, 131
Ben's, 195
Berlin, Irving, 27, 158, 199, 206-8
Boca Raton Museum of Art, 172
Broward County, 9-10, 15, 40, 42-46, 48, 109, 145-46, 150, 152, 155, 157, 159, 163-64, 171, 173

Café Cinematheque, 13, 172-73
Capitman, Barbara, 40-41, 48, 57, 61, 199, 204-5
cemeteries, 125, 157
Chabad Houses, 81
Civil War, 19-20
Clematis Street, 45, 171, 188
Coconut Grove, 110, 139
Cohen, Isidor, 22-23
Collins, John, 25
Cuba, 9, 15, 18, 20-22, 36, 38-39, 42-43, 46-47, 83, 91, 104, 122, 127, 129, 131-32, 134, 201-2, 204
Cuban Hebrew Congregation, 39, 82

David's Bakery, 107
Deering, Charles, 137
Deering Estate at Cutler, 110, 137
Deering, James, 134-36
delis, 10, 15, 30, 43, 48, 69-70, 94, 100, 129, 141, 146, 167, 195

eateries, 72, 77, 91, 93, 105, 141, 167, 195
Eden Roc Hotel, 96, 98
Espanola Way, 51, 79, 91
Evergreen Cemetery, 150, 153, 157

Field, Elnathan, 25
Fisher, Carl, 25-26, 29, 40, 46, 80, 201
Flagler Museum, 171, 190, 192
Florida Atlantic University, 10, 13, 172
Fontainebleau Hotel, 51, 84, 97
Frost Museum of Science, 110
Frost, Phillip, 84, 111, 199, 205-6

Goldstein's Prime, 105-7
Great Depression, 130, 192

Hebrew Home of South Beach, 65-66
historic synagogues, 102
HistoryMiami Museum, 133
Hohauser, Henry, 52, 61-62, 64
Holocaust, 9-10, 13, 15, 34, 36,

47-48, 60, 85, 88, 102, 146-49, 175, 182
Holocaust Documentation and Education Center, 10, 146
Holocaust Memorial, 85, 88
Horowitz, Leonard, 41, 62, 64, 70, 205
hotels, 61, 96

Jacksonville, 23, 31
Jean's Candy Shop, 67
Jewish Community Centers, 68, 96, 115, 172
Jewish Museum of Florida, 13, 47-48, 52, 54, 59, 199, 208-9
Joe's Stone Crab Restaurant, 72

Katz, Moe, 45, 145, 153, 157
Key West, 17, 24

Lansky, Meyer, 36, 54, 201-2, 204
Las Olas Boulevard, 145, 150-51, 153
Levy, Moses, 17
Lincoln Road, 26, 30-31, 67, 70, 80-82, 92
Little Havana, 109-10, 126, 129, 130-31
Lord Balfour Hotel, 62
Lum, Charles, 25
Lum, Henry, 25

Mariel boat lifts, 42, 56, 83, 122, 134
Mediterranean revival, 48-49, 51, 58, 64, 71, 122, 135
Miami, 22-24, 26, 28-29, 31, 34, 36, 38, 40, 42-44, 51-52, 57, 72, 109-10, 114, 116-18, 122, 125-26, 128, 133-34, 137, 139-42, 152, 171, 204

Miami Beach, 10, 13, 25-26, 28-32, 34, 36-37, 40-44, 46-49, 51-52, 57-59, 61-72, 76, 78-81, 83-86, 89, 91-92, 95-97, 100, 103, 129, 191, 199-201, 204-6
Miami-Dade County, 9-10, 15, 32, 44, 66, 109, 136-37, 140, 145, 171
Miami Design District, 139
Miami Design Preservation League, 10, 40, 48, 57, 204
Miami Modern (MiMo), 51, 58, 80, 100
museums, 52, 89
Myerson, Bess, 54-55, 199, 208-9

Nemo Hotel, 63-64
New World Center, 89

Osborn, Ezra, 25

Palm Beach, 22-23, 31, 44, 116, 172-73, 182, 197
Palm Beach County, 9-10, 15, 40, 42-44, 46, 48, 109, 146
Pensacola, 31
Perez Art Museum, 110-11
Ponce de Leon, Juan, 15
Prime 112 Restaurant, 76
Pumpernik's, 79, 99-100

Rascal's, 48
Riverside, 126-27, 129
Roasters and Toasters, 93
Rubell Family Collection, 113

Schneidman, Jake, 22-23
Sephardic Jews, 9, 16-17, 20, 32, 38-39, 104, 118
Shenandoah, 109, 117, 126-27, 129
Sholtz, David, 31
Singer, Sam, 22

Soref Jewish Community Center, 150
Sterling's Men and Boys Store, 145
Stranahan House, 45, 152, 164
synagogues, 82, 95, 116, 140, 182

Tallahassee, 31
Temple Beth David, 13, 110, 116, 120
Temple Beth Shalom, 95, 186, 188
Temple Emanuel, 146
Temple Emanu-El, 83-85, 153-54, 157, 183, 185
Temple Israel, 13, 37, 110, 117, 119, 184, 187-88, 197
Temple Judea, 140
Temple Menorah, 38, 102
Temple Moses, 39, 104

Versace, Gianni, 71
Vizcaya, 51, 110, 134-37

Wahnish, Alfred, 20
Way, Samuel Yulee, 31
Weiss, Rose, 67, 199-201
West Palm Beach, 169, 171, 175, 184
Wolfie's, 48, 79, 99-100, 102
Wolfsonian Museum, 59
Wolfson, Mitchell, 59, 129
World Erotic Art Museum, 60
World War II, 65, 79, 118, 130, 149, 156, 171, 182, 184, 187, 192, 202

Yulee, David Levy, 19, 31, 199-200